Dick Publisher

The Emerald

Book of Irish melodies

Dick Publisher

The Emerald
Book of Irish melodies

ISBN/EAN: 9783744740579

Printed in Europe, USA, Canada, Australia, Japan

Cover: Foto ©Thomas Meinert / pixelio.de

More available books at **www.hansebooks.com**

THE EMERALD;

OR,

BOOK OF IRISH MELODIES.

A CHOICE COLLECTION OF

SENTIMENTAL, COMIC, CONVIVIAL, POLITICAL, AND PATRIOTIC SONGS OF ERINIA.

NEW YORK:
DICK & FITZGERALD, PUBLISHERS,
18 ANN STREET.

CONTENTS.

4   CONTENTS.

THE

EMERALD SONGSTER.

PART I.

The Four-Leaved Shamrock.

[A four-leaved Shamrock is of such rarity that it is supposed to indue the finder with magic power.]

I'll seek a four-leaved shamrock in all the fairy dells,
And if I find the charmed leaves, oh, how I'll weave
    my spells!
I would not waste my magic might on diamond, pearl,
    or gold,
For treasure tires the weary sense—such triumph is
    but cold;
But I would play the enchanter's part in casting bliss
    around—
Oh! not a tear nor aching heart should in the world
    be found.

To worth I would give honor!—I'd dry the mourner's
    tears,
And to the pallid lip recall the smile of happier years;
And hearts that had been long estranged, and friends
    that had grown cold,
Should meet again—like parted streams—and mingle
    as of old!
Oh! thus I'd play the enchanter's part, thus scatter
    bliss around,
And not a tear nor aching heart should in the world
    be found!

The heart that had been mourning o'er vanish'd
    dreams of love
Should see them all returning, like Noah's faithful
    dove,
And Hope should launch her blessed bark on Sorrow's
    dark'ning sea,
And Mis'ry's children have an Ark, and saved from
    sinking be ;
Oh! thus I'd play the enchanter's part, thus scatter
    bliss around,
And not a tear nor aching heart should in the world
    be found.

My Heart's in Old Ireland.

My bark on the billow dash'd gloriously on,
And glad were the notes of the sailor-boy's song ;
Yet sad was my bosom and bursting with woe,
For my heart's in old Ireland wherever I go,
Oh! my heart's in old Ireland wherever I go.

More dear than the flowers that Italy yields,
Are the red-breasted daisies that spangle thy fields.
The shamrock, the hawthorn, the white blossom sloe,
For my heart's in old Ireland wherever I go,
       Oh! my heart's, &c.

The shores they look lovely, yet cheerless and vain,
Bloom the lillies of France, and the olives of Spain ;
When I think of the fields where the wild daisies grow,
Then my heart's in old Ireland wherever I go,
       Oh! my heart's, &c.

The lillies and roses abandon the plains,
Though the summer's gone by, still the shamrock
    remains,
Like a friend in misfortune it blossoms o'er the snow ;
For my heart's in old Ireland wherever I go,
       Oh! my heart's &c.

I sigh and I vow, if e'er I get home,
No more from my dear native cottage I'll roam ;
The harp shall resound, and the goblet shall flow,
For my heart's in old Ireland wherever I go,
Oh! my heart's, &c.

The Green Bushes.

I'll buy you new bavers and fine silken gowns,
I'll buy you new petticoats, flounced to the ground,
If you will prove constant and loyal to me,
And leave your own true love, and follow with me.

I care not for bavers or fine silken hose,
For I am not so poor as to marry for clothes ;
But if you prove constant and loyal to me,
I will leave my own true love, and follow with thee.

Oh! let us be going, young man, if you please,
Oh! let us be going from under these trees,
For my true love is coming—'Tis yonder, I see,
Down by the green bushes where he thinks to meet me.

And when that he found his true love she was flown,
He stood, like a lambkin that blates, all alone ;
For my true love is gone, and she's forsaken me,
Adieu! the green bushes, forever, says he.

The Old Country Party.

BY HARRY M. PALMER.

AIR—Irishman's Shanty.

Say, did ye iver go till an ould country party,
Where the boys are so gay, and the girls dress so
smartly,
While around the turf fire the ould folks take their aise
And a drop of the crater whiniver they please.
Arrah, me jewel! oh! Ireland's the country for me.

The first one I wint to, before I left home,
Was give be me Uncle that lived at Athlone.
He sint word for me to be there without fail,
So I wint in the stage coach that carried the mail.
Arrah, &c.

Whin I opened the door, what a sight met my eyes:
Hot bacon and praties,.wid herrin and pies,
While up on the closet, by way of a lunch,
Was a five gallon bowl full of hot whisky punch.
Arrah, &c.

There was Dolan, the blacksmith, the cooper, McFail,
Wid schoolmaster Casey, and Father O'Neal,
O'Brian, the butcher, wid a great many more,
And the MacEvoy brothers, who came from Bondore.
Arrah, &c.

Thin Biddy McGurn and the brothers O'Neal
Stood up in the floor for a three handed reel.
While, perched on the table, blind piper McGill
Played a tune called "The Little House Under the
Hill."
Arrah, &c.

"The Connaught Man's Rambles" the pipes thin did
play,
While ould folks and young kept dancing away ;
But the music stopped short, for the bottle was dry,
And under the table the piper did lie.
Arrah, &c.

Thin Biddy McClosky sung Kitty Asthore,
And Pat MacEvoy giv us Rory O'More ;
Wid the "Tail of me Coat" by my first cousin Tim,
And "The Life and Adventures of Bryan O'Lynn."
Arrah, &c.

But now I'm away from the folks at Athlone,
As well as me father and mother at home ;
Be the Powers, the tears rushes into me eyes
Whin I think of the whisky, the girls, and the pies.
Arrah, &c.

Pretty Maid Milking her Cow.

It being on a fine summer's morning,
    As birds sweetly tuned on each bough,
I heard a fair maid sing most charming,
    As she sat a milking her cow.
Her voice was enchanting—melodious,
    Which left me scarce able to go ;
My heart it was soothed in solace,
    By the pretty maid milking her cow.

With courtesy I did salute her :
    " Good-morrow, most amiable maid ;
I am your captive slave for the future."
    " Kind sir, do not banter," she said ;
" I am not such a precious rare jewel,
    That I should enamour you so ;
I am but a plain country girl,"
    Said this pretty maid milking her cow.

" The Indies afford no such jewel,
    So precious and transparent clear,
Oh ! do not refuse to be my jewel,
    But consent, and love me, my dear ;
Take pity, and grant my desire,
    And leave me no longer in woe ;
Oh ! love me, or else I'll expire,
    Sweet colleen dhas cruthin amoe.*"

" I don't understand what you mean, sir,
    I never was a slave yet to love ;
These emotions I cannot experience,
    So, I pray, these affections remove ;
To marry, I can assure you,
    That state I will not undergo,
So, young man, I pray you will excuse me,"
    Said this pretty maid milking her cow.

* Pretty maid milking her cow.

" Had I the wealth of great Omar,
    Or all on the African shore ;
Or had I great Devonshire's treasure,
    Or had I ten thousand times more,
Or had I the lamp of Alladin,
    And had I his genius, also—
I'd rather live poor on a mountain,
    With colleen dhas cruthin amoe."

' I beg you, withdraw, and do not tease me,
    I cannot consent unto thee ;
I prefer to live single and airy,
    'Till more of the world I see ;
New cares they would me embarrass—
    Beside, sir, my fortune is low :
Until I get rich I'll not marry,"
    Said the colleen dhas cruthin amoe.

' A young maid is like a ship sailing,
    She don't know how long she may steer,
For in every blast she is in danger,
    So consent, and love me, my dear.
For riches I care not a farthing ;
    Your affections I want, and no more ;
In wedlock I wish to bind you,
    Sweet colleen dhas cruthin amoe !"

The Road of Life ;

Or, Song of the Irish Post-Boy.

Oh ! youth, happy youth ! what a blessing !
    In thy freshness of dawn and of dew ;
When hope the young heart is caressing,
    And our griefs are but light and but few ;
Yet in life, as it swiftly flies o'er us,
    Some musing for sadness we find ;
In youth—we've our troubles before us,
    In age—we leave pleasure behind.

Aye—*Trouble's* the post-boy that drives us
Up hill, till we get to the top;
While Joy's an old servant behind us
We call on forever to stop;
Oh! put on the drag, Joy, my jewel,
As long as the sunset still glows;
Before it is dark 'twould be cruel
To haste to the hill-foot's repose.

But there stands an inn we must stop at,
An extinguisher swings for the sign;
That house is but cold and but narrow—
But the prospect beyond it's divine!
And there—whence there's never returning,
When we travel—as travel we must—
May the gates be all free for our journey!
And the tears of our friends lay the dust!

The Fairy Boy.

[When a beautiful child pines and dies, the Irish peasant believes the healthy
infant has been stolen by the fairies, and a sickly elf left in its place.]

A mother came when stars were paling,
Wailing round a lonely spring;
Thus she cried, while tears were falling,
Calling on the Fairy King:
" Why with spells my child caressing,
Courting him with fairy joy;
Why destroy a mother's blessing,
Wherefore steal my baby boy?

" O'er the mountain, through the wild wood,
Where his childhood loved to play;
Where the flowers are freshly springing,
There I wander day by day.
There I wander, growing fonder
Of the child that made my joy;
On the echoes wildly calling,
To restore my fairy boy.

" But in vain my plaintive calling,
  Tears are falling all in vain ;
He now sports with fairy pleasure,
  He's the treasure of their train.
Fare thee well, my child, for ever,
  In this world I've lost my joy ;
But, in the next, we ne'er shall sever,
  There I'll find my angel boy ! "

I'd Mourn the Hopes.

AIR---The Rose Tree.

I'd mourn the hopes that leave me,
  If thy smiles had left me too ;
I'd weep when friends deceive me,
  Hadst thou been, like them, untrue.

But while I've thee before me,
  With heart so warm, and eyes so bright,
No clouds can linger o'er me,
  That smile turns them all to light.

'Tis not in fate to harm me,
  While fate leaves thy love to me ;
'Tis not in joy to charm me,
  Unless joy be shared with thee.

One Minute's dream about thee
  Were worth a long and endless year
Of waking bliss without thee,
  My own love, my only dear !

And though the hope be gone, love,
  That long sparkled o'er our way,
Oh ! we shall journey on, love,
  More safely without its ray.

Far better lights shall win me,
  Along the path I've yet to roam ;
The mind that burns within me,
  And pure smiles from thee at home.

Thus, when the lamp that lighted
   The traveler, at first goes out,
He feels a while benighted,
   And looks round in fear and doubt.

But soon, the prospect clearing,
   By cloudless starlight on he treads,
And thinks no lamp so cheering
   As that light which heaven sheds !

The Blackbird.

Once on a morning of sweet recreation,
   I heard a fair lady a-making her moan,
With sighing and sobbing, and sad lamentation,
   Aye, singing, "My Blackbird forever is flown!
He's all my heart's treasure, my joy, and my pleasure,
   So justly, my love, my heart follows thee ;
And I am resolved, in foul or fair weather,
   To seek out my Blackbird, wherever he be.

" I will go, a stranger to peril and danger,
   My heart is so loyal in every degree ;
For he's constant and kind, courageous in mind :
   Good luck to my Blackbird, wherever he be !
In Scotland he's loved and dearly approved,
   In England a stranger he seemeth to be ;
But his name I'll advance in Ireland or France,
   Good luck to my Blackbird, wherever he be.

" The birds of the forest are all met together
   The turtle is chosen to dwell with the dove,
And I am resolved, in foul or fair weather,
   Once in the spring-time to seek out my love.
But since fickle Fortune, which still proves uncertain,
   Hath caused this parting between him and me,
His right I'll proclaim, and who dares me blame?
   Good luck to my Blackbird, wherever he be."

The White Cockade.

King Charles he is King James's son,
And from a royal line is sprung ;
Then up with shout, and out with blade,
And we'll raise once more the white cockade.
O ! my dear, my fair-hair'd youth,
Thou yet hast hearts of fire and truth ;
Then up with shout, and out with blade—
We'll raise once more the white cockade

My young men's hearts are dark with woe ;
On my virgin's cheeks the grief-drops flow ;
The sun scarce lights the sorrowing day,
Since our rightful prince went far away ;
He's gone, the stranger holds his throne ;
The royal bird far off is flown :
But up with shout, and out with blade—
We'll stand or fall with the white cockade.

No more the cuckoo hails the spring,
The woods no more with the stanch-hounds ring ;
The song from the glen, so sweet before,
Is hush'd since Charles has left our shore.
The prince is gone : but he soon will come,
With trumpet sound, and with beat of drum ;
Then up with shout, and out with blade—
Huzza for the right and the white cockade.

The Green Linnet.

Curiosity bore a young native of Erin,
  To view the gay banks of the Rhine,
When an empress he saw, and the robe she was wearing
  All over with diamonds did shine ;
A goddess in splendor was never yet seen,
To equal this fair one so mild and serene,
In soft murmur she says, My sweet linnet so green,
  Are you gone—will I never see you more ?

The cold, lofty Alps you freely went over,
  Which nature had placed in your way,
That Marengo, Saloney, around you did hover,
  And Paris did rejoice the next day.
It grieves me the hardships you did undergo,
Over mountains you traveled all covered with snow,
The balance of power your courage laid low,
  Are you gone—will I never see you more?

The crowned heads of Europe when you were in
    splendor,
  Fain would they have you submit,
But the goddess of Freedom soon bid them surrender
  And lowered the standard to your wit;
Old Frederick's colors in France you did bring,
Yet his offspring found shelter under your wing,
That year in Virginia you sweetly did sing,
  Are you gone—will I never see you more?

That numbers of men are eager to slay you,
  Their malice you viewed with a smile,
Their gold through all Europe they sowed to betray you,
  And they joined the Mamelukes on the Nile.
Like ravens for blood their vile passions did burn,
The orphans they slew, and caused the widows to
    mourn,
They say my linnet's gone, and ne'er will return,
  Is he gone—will I never see him more?

When the trumpet of war the grand blast was sounding,
  You marched to the north with good will,
To relieve the poor slaves in their vile sack clothing,
  You used your exertion and skill.
You spread out the wings of your envied train,
While tyrants great Cæsar's old nest set in flames,
Their own subjects they caused to eat herbs on the plains,
  Are you gone—will I never see you more?

In great Waterloo, where numbers laid sprawling,
  In every field, high or low,
Fame on her trumpets through Frenchmen was calling,
  Fresh laurels to place on her brow.

Usurpers did tremble to hear the loud call,
The third old Babe's new buildings did fall,
The Spaniards their fleet in the harbor did call,
    Are you gone—will I never see you more.

I'll roam through the desserts of wild Abyssinia,
    And yet find no cure for my pain,
Will I go and inquire in the isle of St. Helena?
    No, we will whisper in vain.
Tell me, you critics, now tell me in time,
The nation I will range my sweet linnet to find,
Was he slain at Waterloo, or Elba on the Rhine?
    If he was, I will never see him more.

Irish Tinker's Lament.

[Words and music by Mr. W. J. FLORENCE, and sung by him in his great
drama of "Uncle Mike's Cabin; or, The Gipsey's Warning."]

Ted Rooney's my name, from Dublin I came,
    To make my fortune in this quarter ;
With stove in my hand, I'm a tinker so grand,
    But I'm sorry I crassed o'er the water !
        [SPOKEN.] Any tin ware to mend ?

I've been in each town, but there's none like my own,
    I've courted many a gintleman's daughter ;
I've been offered the hand of the fair and the grand,
    Still I'm sorry I crassed o'er the water !
        [SPOKEN.] Any tin ware to mend ?

The fair girl at home, whom I left for to roam,
    Has been led like a lamb to the slaughter :
Ould Hogan she wed—she'd better be dead !
    Och ! I'm sorry I crassed o'er the water !
        [SPOKEN.] Any tin ware to mend ?

She was a fine girrul, every hair was a curl,
    That grew on the spot it had oughter ;
Her cheeks were as red as the hair of her head—
    Faith, I'm sorry I crassed o'er the water !
        [SPOKEN.] Any tin ware to mend ?

Should I ever go home, ne'er again would I roam,
But would live like a true Irish sporter ;
When ould Hogan was dead, his widow I'd wed,
And keep on the right side of the water !
[SPOKEN.] Any tin ware to mend?

Norah, the Pride of Kildare.

As beauteous as Flora is charming young Norah,
The joy of my heart and the Pride of Kildare,
I ne'er will deceive her, for sadly 'twould grieve her,
To find that I sighed for another less fair.

CHORUS :

Her heart with truth teeming, her eye with smiles
beaming,
What mortal could injure a blossom so fair,
Oh, Norah, dear Norah, the Pride of Kildare.

Where'er I may be, love, I'll ne'er forget thee, love,
Though beauties may smile and try to ensnare,
Yet nothing shall ever my heart from thine sever,
Dear Norah, sweet Norah, the Pride of Kildare.
Her heart, &c.

The Irish Brigade O!

Oh ! why should I sing of Roman or Greek,
The boys we hear tell of in story ?
Come, match me, for fighting, for frolic, or freak,
An Irishman reigning in glory.
There's Ajax and Hector, and bold Agamemnon,
Were up to the tricks of our trade O,
But the rollickin' boys for war, women, and noise,
Are the boys of the Irish Brigade O !

What for would I sing of Helen of Troy,
  Or the mischief that came of her flirting?
Sure, there's Biddy O'Flannigan, pride of Forroy,
  Twice as much of an Helen, that's certain.
Then for Venus, Minerva, or Queen Cleopatra,
  Bad luck to the word shall be said O!
But the rollickin' boys for war, women, and noise,
  Are the boys of the Irish Brigade O!

What for would I sing ye of classical fun,
  Of games, boys, Olympic or Parthian?
And the Curragh's the course where the knowing
    ones done,
  And there's Mallow, that flogs for diversion.
For fighting, for drinking, for females and all,
  No times like our times e'er were made O!
For the rollickin' boys, for war, women, and noise,
  Are the boys of the Irish Brigade O!

Savourneen Deelish.

Ah! the moment was sad when my love and I parted—
      Savourneen deelish Eileen oge!*
As I kissed off her tears I was nigh broken-hearted—
      Savourneen deelish Eileen oge!
Wan was her cheek which hung on my shoulder—
Damp was her hand, no marble was colder,
I felt that again I should never behold her.
      Savourneen deelish Eileen oge!

When the word of command put our men into motion,
      Savourneen deelish Eileen oge!
I buckled on my knapsack to cross the wide ocean,
      Savourneen deelish Eileen oge!
Brisk were our troops, all roaring like thunder,
Pleased with the voyage, impatient for plunder,
My bosom with grief was almost torn asunder.
      Savourneen deelish Eileen oge!

------
* Darling dear Young Ellen.

Long I fought for my country, far, far from my true love,
    Savourneen deelish Eileen oge !
All my pay and my bounty I hoarded for you, love
    Savourneen deelish Eileen oge !
Peace was proclaimed—escaped from the slaughter,
Landed at home, my sweet girl I sought her ;
But sorrow, alas ! to the cold grave had brought her.
    Savourneen deelish Eileen oge !

The Low-backed Car.

[The words and music of this Song, with Piano-forte accompaniment, are pub
lished by Wm. Hall & Son, New York.]

When first I saw sweet Peggy,
  'Twas on a market day,
A low-backed car she drove, and sat
  Upon a truss of hay ;
But when that hay was blooming grass,
  And decked with flowers of Spring,
No flow'r was there that could compare
  With the blooming girl I sing :
As she sat in the low-backed car—
The man at the turnpike bar
  Never asked for the toll,
  But just rubbed his owld poll,
And looked after the low-backed car.

In battle's wild commotion,
  The proud and mighty Mars,
With hostile scythes, demands his tithes
  Of death--in warlike cars ;
While Peggy, peaceful goddess,
  Has darts in her bright eye,
That knocked men down, in the market town
  As right and left they fly—
While she sits in her low-backed car,
Than battle more dangerous far—
  For the doctor's art
  Cannot cure the heart
That is hit from that low-backed car.

Sweet Peggy, round her car, sir,
　Has strings of ducks and geese.
But the scores of hearts she slaughters
　By far out-number these ;
While she among her poultry sits,
　Just like a turtle dove,
Well worth the cage, I do engage,
　Of the blooming god of love—
While she sits in the low-backed car,
The lovers come near and far,
　　And envy the chicken
　　Thet Peggy is pickin',
As she sits in the low-backed car.

Oh ! I'd rather own that car, sir,
　With Peggy by my side,
Than a coach-and-four and goold galore,
　And a lady for my bride ;
For the lady would sit forninst me,
　On a cushion made with taste,
While Peggy would sit beside me,
　With my arm around her waist—
While we drove in the low-backed car,
To be married by Father Mahar,
　　Oh ! my heart would beat high
　　At her glance and her sigh—
Though it beat in a low-backed car.

Molly Bawn.

O, Molly Bawn, why leave me pining,
　Or lonely waiting here for you—
While the stars above are brightly shining,
　Because they have nothing else to do.
The flowers late were open keeping,
　To try a rival blush with you,
But their mother, Nature, kept them sleeping,
　With their rosy faces wash'd in dew.
　　　　　O, Molly, &c.

The pretty flowers were made to bloom, dear,
   And the pretty stars were made to shine ;
The pretty girls were made for the boys, dear,
   And may be you were made for mine.
The wicked watch-dog here is snarling—
   He takes me for a thief, d'ye see ?
For he knows I'd steal you, Molly, darling,
   And then transported I should be.
              O, Molly, &c.

Angels' Whisper.

   A baby was sleeping,
   Its mother was weeping,
For her husband was far on the wide raging sea,
   And the tempest was swelling
   'Round the fisherman's dwelling,
And she cried, " Dermont, darling, oh ! come back
     to me !"

   Her beads while she number'd,
   The baby still slumber'd,
And smiled in her face as she bended her knee :
   " Oh ! bless'd be that warning,
   My child, thy sleep adorning,
For I know that the angels are whispering to thee.

   "And while they are keeping
   Bright watch o'er thy sleeping,
Oh ! pray to them softly, my baby, with me—
   And say thou wouldst rather
   They'd watch o'er thy father,
For I know that the angels are whispering with
     thee."

   The dawn of the morning
   Saw Dermot returning,
And the wife wept with joy her babe's father to see ;
   And closely caressing
   Her child, with a blessing,
Said, " I knew that the angels were whispering with
     thee."

Lament of the Irish Emigrant.

I'm sitting on the stile, Mary,
  Where we sat side by side,
On a bright May morning long ago,
  When first you were my bride ;
The corn was springing fresh and green,
  And the lark sang loud and high,
And the red was on thy lip, Mary,
  And the love light in your eye.

The place is little changed, Mary,
  The day is bright as then ;
The lark's loud song is in my ear,
  And the corn is green again !
But I miss the soft clasp of your hand,
  And your breath warm on my cheek,
And I still keep list'ning for the words
  You never more may speak.

'Tis but a step down yonder lane,
  And the little church stands near—
The church where we were wed, Mary,
  I see the spire from here ;
But the graveyard lies between, Mary,
  And my step might break your rest,
For I've laid you, darling, down to sleep,
  With your baby on your breast.

I'm very lonely now, Mary,
  For the poor make no new friends,
But, O ! they love thee better far,
  The few our father sends;
And you were all I had, Mary,
  My blessing and my pride ;
There's nothing left to care for now,
  Since my poor Mary died.

I'm bidding you a long farewell,
  My Mary, kind and true,
But I'll not forget you, darling,
  In the land I'm going to ;

They say there's bread and work for all,
  And the sun shines always there,
But I'll not forget old Ireland,
  Were it fifty times as fair.

And often in those grand old woods,
  I'll sit and shut my eyes,
And my heart will travel back again,
  To the place where Mary lies ;
And I'll think I see the little stile
  Where we sat side by side,
And the springing corn, and bright May morn,
  When first you were my bride.

Heigh for the Petticoat.

Och ! a petticoat, honey, is an Irishman's joy,
  Go where he will, his time merrily passes ;
Search the world over, sure Paddy's the boy,
  For banging the men and for kissing the lasses ;
And if you but get a red coat to your back,
  In Russia, in Prussia, in France, or in Flanders,
All the pretty ma'amselles have a mighty neat knack
  Of cocking their chins both at men and commanders.
Then heigh for the petticoat, that is the joy,
  Go where I will my time merrily passes ;
Search the world over, sure Paddy's the boy,
  For banging the men, and for kissing the lasses.

When sweet Kitty Conner pierced me clean through
      the heart,
  And chose Teddy Blarney, a big man of honor,
One moonshiny night, to give ease to my smart,
  I kicked Mr. Blarney, and kissed Mrs. Conner.
And the little plump god, for his mother knew what,
  Was the son of old Mars, or he'd never alarm ye ;
And if he'd be growing as tall as he's fat,
    You'd see Mr. Cupid brought up to the army.
      Then heigh for the petticoat, &c.

The Shan Van Vogh. °

[A Ballad of 1796.]

Oh ! the French are on the sea,
  Says the Shan Van Vogh ;
The French are on the sea,
  Says the Shan Van Vogh ;
Oh ! the French are in the Bay,
They'll be here without delay,
And the Orange will decay,
  Says the Shan Van Vogh.
      Oh ! the French are in the Bay,
      They'll be here by break of day,
      And the Orange will decay,
        Says the Shan Van Vogh.

And where will they have their camp?
  Says the Shan Van Vogh ;
Where will they have their camp ?
  Says the Shan Van Vogh :
On the Curragh of Kildare,
The boys they will be there,
With their pikes in good repair,
  Says the Shan Van Vogh.
      To the Curragh of Kildare
      The boys they will repair,
      And Lord Edward will be there,
        Says the Shan Van Vogh.

Then what will the yeomen do?
  Says the Shan Van Vogh ;
What will the yeomen do?
  Says the Shan Van Vogh ;
What should the yeomen do,
But throw off the red and blue,
And swear that they'll be true
  To the Shan Van Vogh?
          What should, &c.

° Properly spelt, An t-sean bhean bhochd, meaning The Poor Old Woman—
another name for Ireland.

And what color will they wear?
　Says the Shan Van Vogh ;
What color will they wear?
　Says the Shan Van Vogh ;
What color should be seen
Where our fathers' homes have been,
But their own immortal Green?
　Says the Shan Van Vogh.
　　　　　What color, &c.

And will Ireland then be free?
　Says the Shan Van Vogh ;
Will Ireland then be free?
　Says the Shan Van Vogh.
Yes! Ireland SHALL be free,
From the centre to the sea;
Then hurra for Liberty!
　Says the Shan Van Vogh.
　　　　　Yes! Ireland, &c.

Aggie Asthore.

[By permission of J. H. HIDLEY, Albany, N. Y., publisher and proprietor of the copyright Sung by W. J. FLORENCE, and always received with shouts of applause.]

Oh! blessings for ever on Aggie Asthore,
She's good as she's lovely, and twenty times more.
With her sparkling blue eyes and her eloquent smile ;
Och! the hearts of the hardest 'tis she can beguile.
　Oh! blessings on Erin's fair maid I adore,
　She's good as she's lovely, my Aggie Asthore.

The first time we met 'twas at our village fair,
And the prettiest girls of the country were there,
But never did I see, either since or before,
One fit to be named with my Aggie Asthore--Aggie
　　dear.
　　　　　Oh! blessing on Erin's, &c.

I asked her to dance, and 'twas then with the pride
I stood out on the floor, my sweet girl by my side ;
But oh ! how I sighed when we gave up the floor,
Shure my heart was clane gone to dear Aggie Asthore
    --Aggie dear.
                    Oh ! blessing on Erin's, &c.

My love it is faithful and honest and true,
And much more than that, 'tis a winning love, too,
For the day will come round, with the ring to the
    "fore."
When for life she is mine, my dear Aggie Asthore—
        Aggie dear.
                    Oh ! blessing on Erin's, &c.

———

Paddy Goshlow.

BY G. W. ANDERSON.

AIR---Billy Barlow.

My darling, don't smile, while to you I do tell
The very sad fate that to me has befell :
I was crossing the street, to come here, ah ! oh !
And slap into the gutter went Paddy Goshlow.
    With me hi ho, Paddy Goshlow,
    Slap into the gutter went Paddy Goshlow.

I've a note which the President sent me, so fine ;
He axed me quite dacent to go wid him and dine ;
He said that the company ne'er could agree,
Without the pleasure of my company.
    With me hi ho, Paddy Goshlow, &c.

I arrived at the house, and I looked mighty glum ;
The President said, " Why, we thought you'd ne'er
    come."
Says I, " Me clothes are all torn, and that yez all
    know,
And a bashful ould fellow is Paddy Goshlow."
    With me hi ho, Paddy Goshlow, &c.

I was next introduced to the company fair,
Whin a lady stood by me, with such sweet auburn
  hair.
She seized hold of my hand, and shook it just so,
" Let go, you ould divil," cried Paddy Goshlow.
  With me hi ho, Paddy Goshlow.

I left the company all in despair ;
The women went crazy, and tore all their hair,
They fell on their knees, and cried out oh ! oh !
' Don't leave the dear company, Paddy Goshlow."
  With me hi ho, Paddy Goshlow, &c.

I was on my way home, on a moonlighted night,
Far away in the distance I saw a beautiful sight :
A crowd of young spalpeens had collected, just so,
To take a good peep at Paddy Goshlow.
  With me hi ho, Paddy Goshlow, &c.

I arrived at the house, and so as to be sure,
I sat on a tub, just close by the dure ;
I got asleep on the edge, and it's in I fell, oh !
And here's the drowned remains of poor Paddy
  Goshlow.
  With me hi ho, Paddy Goshlow,
  Here's the drowned remains of poor Paddy
  Goshlow.

Kitty Tyrrell.

You're looking as fresh as the morn, darling,
  You're looking as bright as the day ;
But while on your charms I'm dilating,
  You're stealing my poor heart away.
But keep it and welcome, mavourneen,
  Its loss I'm not going to mourn ;
Yet one heart's enough for a body,
  So pray give me yours in return,
    Mavourneen, mavourneen,
O ! pray give me yours in return.

I've built me a neat little cot, darling,
  I've pigs and potatoes in store ;
I've twenty good pounds in the bank, love,
  And may be, a pound or two more.
It's all very well to have riches,
  But I'm such a covetous elf,
I can't help still sighing for something,
  And, darling, that something's yourself,
    Mavourneen, mavourneen,
And that something you know, is yourself.

You're smiling, and that's a good sign, darling,
  Say "yes," and you'll never repent,
Or, if you would rather be silent,
  Your silence I'll take for consent.
That good natured dimple's a tell-tale,
  Now all that I have is your own ;
This week you may be Kitty Tyrrell,
  Next week you'll be Mistress Malone,
    Mavourneen, mavourneen,
You'll be my own Mistress Malone.

I'm Leaving Old Ireland.

I'm leaving old Ireland,
  The land of my heart,
Oh ! bless me, dear mother,
  Before I depart ;
I know you will miss me,
  I fear you will grieve,
When darkly between us
  The dark waters heave ;
But heaven will watch o'er you
  And kindly befriend,
And still your poor Kathleen
  From danger defend.
    I'm leaving old Ireland,
    The land of my heart,
    Oh ! bless me, dear mother,
    Before I depart.

When far among strangers,
  I wander alone,
My thoughts will be straying
  To days that are gone ;
Asleep or awaking,
  I'll think of you still,
And our turf-covered cabin,
  Beside the green hill ;
The hour will be joyous
  And welcome to me,
When after long absence
  My dear home I see.
    I'm leaving old Ireland,
    The land of my heart,
    Oh ! bless me, dear mother,
    Before I depart.

The Gray Mare.

As I was a walking to Nottingham fair,
A riding on horseback upon a gray mare,
The mare it was black, but the divil a hair
But what was all yaller, upon the grey mare.

There was the King, the Queen, and a couple of more,
A riding on horseback, a walking before ;
The bells did ring and the people did stare,
To see a coach and six horses drawn by a gray mare.

It rained and it snowed, I stood out in the storm
With my hat in my hand to keep my head warm ;
The mare threw me into the ditch, but I mounted
      again,
And on my tiptoes rode o'er the plain.

I'll saddle the mare and to fishing I'll go,
To fishing I'll go, whether or no ;
If my wagon upsets and my fish it would spill,
I'll sell the gray mare, I'll be d——d if I will.

The Exile of Erin.

There came to the beach a poor exile of Erin,
　The dew on his robe was heavy and chill ;
For his country he sighed, when, at twilight repairing,
　To wander alone by the wind-beaten hill.
But the day-star attracted his eye's sad devotion.
For it rose on his own native isle of the ocean,
Where once, in the flow of his youthful emotion,
　He sang the bold anthem of Erin go bragh.

"Oh, sad is my fate," said the heart-broken stranger,
　" The wild deer and wolf to a covert can flee,
But I have no refuge from famine or danger,
　A home and a country remains not for me !
Ah ! never again, in the green shady bower,
Where my forefather's lived, shall I spend the sweet
　　hours,
Or cover my harp with the wild woven flowers,
　And strike the sweet numbers of Erin go bragh !

"Oh, Erin, my country ! though sad and forsaken,
　In dreams I visit thy sea-beaten shore ;
But alas ! in a far foreign land I awaken,
　And sigh for the friends that can meet me no
　　more ;
And thou, cruel fate ! wilt thou never replace me
In a mansion of peace, where no perils can chase me ?
Ah ! never again shall my brothers embrace me!
　They died to defend me, or live to deplore.

" Where now is my cabin door, so fast by the wild-
　　wood ?
Sisters and sires did weep for its fall.
Where is the mother that looked on my childhood ?
　And where is my bosom friend—dearer than all ?
Ah ! my sad soul, long abandoned by pleasure !
Why did it doat on a fast fading treasure ?
Tears, like the rain, may fall without measure,
　But rapture and beauty they cannot recall.

" But yet all its fond recollection suppressing,
    One dying wish my fond bosom shall draw ;
Erin ! an exile bequeaths thee his blessing,
    Land of my forefathers, Erin go bragh !
Buried and cold, when my heart stills its motion,
Green be thy fields, sweetest isle in the ocean,
And the harp-striking bards sing aloud with devotion,
    ' Erin mavourneen ! sweet Erin go bragh ! ' "

The Fine Old Irish Gentleman.

I'll sing you a dacent song, made by a Paddy's pate,
Of a raal ould Irish gintleman, who had a fine estate,
Whose mansion it was made of mud, with thatch and
    all complate,
With a hole at top, through which the smoke so grace-
    fully did retrate,
    Hurrah ! for the ould Irish gintleman, the boy of the
        oulden time.

His walls so cold, were cover'd with the devil a thing
    for show,
Except an ould shillelah, which had knocked down
    many a foe,
And there ould Barney sat at ease, without shoes or hose,
And quaffed his noggin of poteen to warm his big red
    nose,
    Like a fine ould Irish gintleman, the boy of the oulden
        time.

To Donnybrook his custom was to go to every fair,
And though he'd seen a few score years, he still was
    young when there,
And while the rich they feasted him, he still, among
    the poor
Would sing, and dance, and hurl, and fight, and make
    the spalpeens roar,
    Like a real ould Irish gintleman, the boy of the
        oulden time.

But och mavrone! once at a row ould Barney got a
    knock,
And one that kilt him, 'cause he couldn't get over the
    shock ;
They laid him out so beautiful, and then set up a groan,
Och ! Barney, darlint, jewel dear, why did you die?
    och, hone !
  Then they waked this Irish gintleman, the boy of the
    oulden time.

Though all things in their course must change, and
    seasons pass away,
Yet Irish hearts of oulden time were just as at this day.
Each Irish boy, he took a pride to prove himself a man,
To serve a friend and bate a foe, it always was the plan
  Of a raal ould Irish gintleman, the boy of the oulden
    time.

The Harp that once thro' Tara's Halls.

The harp that once thro' Tara's halls
    The soul of music shed,
Now hangs as mute on Tara's walls,
    As if that soul were fled.
So sleeps the pride of former days,
    So glory's thrill is o'er,
And hearts that once beat high for praise,
    Now feel that pulse no more.

No more to chiefs and ladies bright,
    The harp of Tara swells ;
The chord alone, that breaks at night,
    Its tale of ruin tells.
Thus freedom now but seldom wakes ;
    The only throb she gives,
Is when some heart indignant breaks,
    To show that still she lives.

Doran's Ass.

One Paddy Doyle lived in Killarney ;
  He courted a girl named Biddy Tool.
His tongue was tipped with a bit of blarney,
  The same to Paddy was a golden rule :
Both day and dawn she was his colleen ;
  When to himself he'd often say :
What need I care, when she's my drolleen,
  A coming to meet me on the way?
          Whack fol de darral ido
          Whack fol de darral lal la.

One heavenly night in last November,
  Paddy went out to meet his love ;
What night it was I don't remember,
  But the moon shone brightly from above.
That day the boy had got some liquor,
  Which made his spirits light and gay ;
Arrah ! what's the use in walking quicker,
  When I know she'll meet me on the way !
          Whack fol de darral, &c.

He tuned his pipes and fell a humming,
  As gently onward he did jog ;
But fatigue and whisky overcame him,
  So Paddy lay down upon the sod.
He was not long without a comrade,
  One that could kick up the hay ;
For a big jackass soon smelt out Paddy,
  And lay down beside him on the way.
          Whack fol de darral, &c.

As Pat lay there in gentle slumbers,
  Thinking of his Biddy dear,
He dreamt of pleasures without numbers
  A coming on the ensuing year.
He spread his arms out on the grass,
  His spirits felt so light and gay ;
But instead of Biddy, he gripped the ass,
  Roaring out : I have her anyway.
          Whack fol de darral, &c.

He hugged and smugged his hairy messer,
  And flung his hat to worldly care ;
Says Pat : she's mine, and may heaven bless her,
  But oh ! be me soul, she's like a bear.
He put his hands on the donkey's nose,
  With that the ass began to bray ;
Pat jumped up, and roared out :
  Who sarved me in such a way?
        Whack fol de darral, &c.

Pat ran home as fast as he could,
  At railway speed, or as fast, I'm sure.
He never stopped a leg or foot,
  Until he came to Biddy's door.
By that time 'twas getting morning—
  Down on his knees he fell to pray,
Crying : let me in, my Biddy darling,
  I'm kilt, I'm murdered on the way.
        Whack fol de darral, &c.

He told her his story mighty civil,
  While she prepared a whisky glass—
How he hugged and smugged the hairy divil.
  Go along, says she. 'twas Doran's ass.
I know it was, my Biddy darling.
  They both got married the very next day,
But he never got back his ould straw hat,
  That the jackass ate up on the way.
        Whack fol de darral, &c.

The Wonderful Irishman.

There was a lady lived at Leith,
  A lady very stylish, man,
And yet in spite of her teeth,
  She fell in love with an Irishman --
    A nasty, ugly Irishman,
    A wild, tremendous Irishman—
A tearing, swearing, thumping, bumping, ramping,
  roaring Irishman.

His face was no ways beautiful,
   For with small-pox 'twas scarred across,
And the shoulders of the ugly dog
   Were almost double a yard across.
     O the lump of an Irishman,
     The whiskey-devouring Irishman—
The great he rogue, with his wonderful brogue, the
   fighting, rioting Irishman.

One of his eyes was bottle-green,
   And the other was out, my dear,
And the calves of his wicked-looking legs
   Were more than two feet across, my dear.
     O the great big Irishman,
     The rattling, battling Irishman—
The stamping, ramping, swaggering, staggering, lath-
   ering, swash of an Irishman.

He took so much of Lundy foot
   That he used to snort and snuffle, O,
And in shape and size the fellow's neck
   Was as bad as the neck of a buffalo.
     O the horrible Irishman,
     The thundering, blundering Irishman—
The slashing, dashing, smashing, lashing, thrashing,
   hashing Irishman.

His name was a terrible name, indeed,
   Being Timothy Thady Mulligan;
And whenever he emptied his tumbler of punch,
   He'd not rest till he filled it full again.
     Th' intoxicated Irishman—
     The boozing, bruizing Irishman—
The whisky, frisky, rummy, grummy, brandy, no-
   dandy Irishman.

This was the lad the lady loved,
   Like all the girls of quality,
And he broke the skulls of the men of Leith
   Just by way of jollity;
     O the slathering Irishman,
     The barbarous, savage Irishman—
The hearts of the maids, and the gentlemen's heads,
   were bothered, I'm sure, by this Irishman.

Erin is My Home.

Oh ! I have roam'd in many lands,
    And many friends I've met ;
Not one fair scene or kindly smile
    Can this fond heart forget ;
But I'll confess that I'm content,
    No more I wish to roam ;
Oh ! steer my bark to Erin's isle—
    For Erin is my home.
        Oh ! steer my bark, &c.

If England were my place of birth,
    I'd love her tranquil shore ;
But if Columbia were my home,
    Her freedom I'd adore.
Though pleasant days in both I pass'd,
    I dream of days to come ;
Oh ! steer my bark to Erin's isle—
    For Erin is my home.
        Oh ! steer my bark, &c.

Purty Molly Brallaghan.

Ah ! then, Mam dear, did you ever hear of purty Molly
        Brallaghan ?
Troth, dear, I've lost her, and I'll never be a man again.
Not a spot on my hide will another summer tan again,
    Since Molly she has left me all alone for to die.
The place where my heart was you might easy rowl a
        turnip in,
It's the size of all Dublin, and from Dublin to the
        Devil's glin,
If she chose to take another, sure she might have sent
        mine back agin,
    And not to leave me here all alone for to die.

Mam, dear, I remember when the milking time was
    past and gone,
We went into the meadows where she swore I was the
    only man
That ever she could love—yet oh ! the base, the cruel
    one,
    After all that to leave me here alone for to die!
Mam, dear, I remember as we came home the rain began,
I rowl'd her in my frize coat, tho' the divil a waistcoat I
    had on,
And my shirt was rather fine-drawn ; yet oh ! the base
    and cruel one,
    After all that she's left me here alone for to die.

I went and towld my tale to Father McDonnell, Mam,
And thin I wint and ax'd advice of Counsellor O'Con-
    nell, Mam.
He towld me promise-breaches had been ever since the
    world began,
    Now, I have only one pair, Mam, and they are cor-
      duroy !
Arrah, what could he mean, Mam ? or what would you
    advise me to?
Must my corduroys to Molly go ? in troth, I'm bother'd
    what to do.
I can't afford to lose both my heart and my breeches too,
    Yet what need I care, when I've only to die !

Oh ! the left side of my carcass is as weak as water
    gruel, Mam—
The divil a bit upon my bones since Molly's proved so
    cruel, Mam,
I wish I had a carbine, I'd go and fight a duel, Mam.
    Sure, it's better far to kill myself than stay here to die.
I'm hot and determined as a live Salamander, Mam !
Won't you come to my wake, when I go my long mean-
    der, Mam ?
Oh ! I'll feel myself as valiant as the famous Alexander,
    Mam,
    When I hear yez crying round me, "Arrah, why did
      you die ?"

Kathleen Mavourneen.

Kathleen Mavourneen! the gray dawn is breaking,
The horn of the hunter is heard on the hill,
The lark from her light wing the bright dew is shaking,
Kathleen Mavourneen, what, slumb'ring still?
Ah! hast thou forgotten how soon we must sever?

Oh! hast thou forgotten this day we must part?
It may be for years, and it may be forever,
Oh! why art thou silent, thou voice of my heart?
It may be for years and it may be forever,
Then why art thou silent, Kathleen Mavourneen?

Kathleen Mavourneen! awake from thy slumbers,
The blue mountains glow in the sun's golden light.
Ah! where is the spell that once hung on my numbers,
Arise in thy beauty, thou star of my night,
Arise in thy beauty, thou star of my night,

Mavourneen, Mavourneen, my sad tears are falling,
To think that from Erin and thee I must part,
It may be for years and it may be forever,
Then why art thou silent, thou voice of my heart?
It may be for years, and it may be forever,
Then why art thou silent, Kathleen Mavourneen?

Norah McShane.

I've left Ballymornach a long way behind me,
    To better my fortune I've crossed the big sea ;
But I'm sadly alone, not a creature to mind me,
    And faith I'm as wretched as wretched can be ;
I think of the buttermilk, fresh as the daisy,
    The beautiful halls and the emerald plain,
And, ah! don't I oftentimes think myself crazy,
    About that black-eyed rogue, sweet Norah McShane.

I sigh for the turf-pile so cheerfully burning,
  When barefoot I trudged it from toiling afar,
When I toss'd in the light the thirteen I'd been
      earning,
  And whistled the anthem of "Erin go bragh"
In truth, I believe that I'm half broken-hearted,
  To my country and love I must get back again,
For I've never been happy at all since I parted
  From sweet Ballymornach and Norah McShane.

Oh! there's something so sweet in the cot I was born
      in,
  Though the walls are but mud and the roof is but
      thatch ;
How familiar the grunt of the pigs in the mornin',
  What music in lifting the rusty old latch.
'Tis true I'd no money, but then I'd no sorrow,
  My pockets were light, but my head had no pain ;
And if I but live till the sun shine to-morrow,
  I'll be off to ould Ireland and Norah McShane.

The Captain.

[The music of this song is published by OLIVER DITSON & Co., Boston, by
whose permission we use the words. Words and music by Mr. W. J. FLOR-
ENCE, written expressly for Mrs W. J. FLORENCE, and first sung by her in
all the principal cities of the United States, Great Britain, and Ireland.]

As they marched through the town with their banners
      so gay,
I ran to the window to hear the band play ;
I peeped through the blinds very cautiously then,
Lest the neighbors should say I was looking at the
      men ;
I heard the drums beat, and the music so sweet,
But my eyes at the time had a much greater treat—
The troops were the finest I ever did see,
For the captain with his whisker took a sly glimpse at
      me.

When we met at the ball, I of course thought it right
To pretend that we never had met before that night,
But he knew me at once, I perceived by his glance,
And I hung down my head when he asked me to dance.
He sat by my side at the end of the set,
And the sweet words he spoke I shall never forget.
Yes, the troops were the finest I ever did see,
For the captain with his whisker took a sly glimpse at
    me.

My Nick-name is Barney.

BY G. W. ANDERSON.

AIR---Flaming O'Flannagans.

My nick-name is Barney—och, I'm the divil!
  For teasing the girls, shure, I'm never alone;
For me and myself are always together,
  For plaguing the girls when I'm not at home.
The girl that I had was a swate charmer,
  But nobody knew that she drank ;
The devil couldn't make her marry me,
  Because I'd no money in the bank.

CHORUS :

Rum a-diddle, diddle whack !
For that was the way with Barney, the lover,
  Who would not be leaving the girls all alone,
He took the pattern after his brother,
  For plaguing the girls when he was not at home.

I gave her the sack, and got clear of the charmer,
  Divil the ha'p'orth I think of her now,
Because I fell out with her beast of a mother,
  Who pitched me clean over the sow.
The sow commenced grunting and squealing,
  And the old lady ran to the door ;
She gave me a good smack with the poker,
  Which laid me flat on the floor.
    Rum a-diddle, diddle, &c.

Thanks be to myself, it is now I am married,
  Poor Barney has never led such a life;
For, bless me! I'm always getting the divil
  Of a fine pounding from the hands of my wife.
But, mark me, now, boys, and never get married,
  You always will lade a dreadful hard life;
But should you ever take hold of that notion,
  Take a fine girl, and make her your wife.
    Rum a-diddle, diddle, &c.

The Patriot Mother.

[A ballad of '98.]

" Come, tell us the name of the rebelly crew
  Who lifted the pike on the Curragh with you;
Come, tell us their treason, and then you'll be free,
  Or by heavens, you shall swing from the high gallows
    tree."

" Alanna! alanna! the shadow of shame
  Has never yet fallen upon one of your name,
And, oh! may the food from my bosom you drew,
  In your veins turn to poison, if *you* turn untrue.

" The foul words—oh! let them not blacken your
    tongue,
That would prove to your friends and your country a
    wrong,
Or the curse of a mother, so bitter and dread,
  With the wrath of the Lord—may they fall on your
    head!

" I have no one but you in the whole world wide,
  Yet, false to your pledge, you'd ne'er stand at my
    side;
If a traitor you liv'd, you'd be farther away
  From my heart than, if true, you were wrapp'd in the
    clay.

* Alaneacht signifies beauty.

" Oh ! deeper and darker the mourning would be
For your falsehood so base, than your death proud
        and free ;
Dearer, far dearer than ever to me,
My darling, you'll be on the brave gallows tree.

" 'Tis holy, agra,* with the bravest and best—
Go, go, from my heart, and be joined with the rest;
Alanna ma chree ! O, alanna ma chree ! †
Sure a ' stag ' ‡ and a traitor you never will be."

There's no look of a traitor upon the young brow
That's raised to the tempters so haughtily now ;
No traitor e'er held up the firm head so high—
No traitor e'er show'd such a proud flashing eye.

On the high gallows tree ! on the brave gallows tree !
Where smiled leaves and blossoms, his sad doom met
        he ;
But it never bore blossoms so pure or so fair,
As the heart of the martyr that hangs from it there.

The New Policeman.

AIR—Nora Creina.

Oh ! good evening, gentlemen, to-day,
    Now list awhile to me and my blarney ;
I am arrived from Dublin quay,
    Now, sure, my name is Michael Karney.
Grub was scarce and luck was bad,
    Hunger's rumbling ne'er did cease, man,
So to this city I came, egad,
    And Murphy's made me a new Policeman.
        Ranting, rollicking Irish joys,
            Always quarreling, ne'er at peace, man,
        Kissing the girls and licking the boys ;
            Oh ! that's the life of a new Policeman.

* My love.   † Beauty of my heart.   ‡ An informer.

Och ! there isn't yard or garden wall,
　About the city but I can scale it,
And if any thing I find at all,
　Now shouldn't I a fool be not to nail it.
Next morning there's a hue and cry,
　There's something stolen and to be brief, man,
Oh ! by the hookey, who but I,
　Am running about to catch the thief, man.

Ranting, rollicking, &c.

And then, you know, when I'm out at night,
　In every hole and corner peeping ;
What's that I spy by the pale moonlight,
　Och ! by my soul, 'tis a gentleman sleeping.
His pockets I grope and his money I take,
　And then with my staff in the ribs I'm jobbing him,
And if by chance the man should wake,
　I tell him I thought a thief was robbing him.

Ranting, rollicking, &c.

Then if there isn't a row in the street,
　Sure, it's myself knows how to raise one,
For I knock the first man down I meet,
　Then make a shindy fit to craze one.
He resists, then loud he hollers—
　I lock him up and swear he's rioty ;
Next morning he is fined two dollars,
　Just because myself couldn't murder him quietly.

Ranting, rollicking, &c.

I'm in with every servant maid,
　For mutton and love I've ever an itching,
And of being caught I'm not afraid,
　For, sure, I'm there to guard the kitchen.
And then, too, don't the Scriptures say,
　Multiply, too, and increase men,
So if we only have our way,
　We'll fill the city with little policemen.

Ranting, rollicking, &c.

Och! Norah Dear.

Och! Norah dear, I'm waiting here,
I'm watching still for you, love ;
And while you sleep, the flow'rets weep,
All shrined in tears of dew, love.
The silv'ry moon, its bright rays soon
Behind the hills will fade, love ;
But better there her beauties bear,
For thou her beams would shade, love.
Och! Norah dear, &c.

Och! Norah dear! I'm waiting here,
The stars look cold and blue, love ;
Their twinkling rays have come to gaze,
To see how bright are you, love.
The breeze that brings such balmy things
From all that's bright and fair, love,
It sighs to sip from thy sweet lip
The perfume that lies there, love.
Och! Norah dear, &c.

Ould Ireland! You're My Darlin'.

Ould Ireland! you're my jewel. sure,
My heart's delight and glory ;
Till time shall pass his empty glass,
Your name shall live in story.
And this shall be the song for me,
The first my heart was larnin',
Before my tongue one accent sung,
Ould Ireland! you're my darlin'.

My blessing's on each manly son
Of thine who will stand by thee ;
But hang the knave and dastard slave
So base as to deny thee.

Then bould and free, while yet for me
  The globe is round us whirlin',
My song shall be, Gra Galmachree,
  Ould Ireland ! you're my darlin' !

Sweet spot of earth that gave me birth,
  Deep in my soul I cherish,
While life remains within these veins,
  A love that ne'er can perish.
If it was a thing that I could sing,
  Like any thrush or starlin',
In cage or tree, my song should be,
  Ould Ireland ! you're my darlin'.

Hibernia's Lovely Jean.

When parting from the Scottish shore
  And the Highland's mossy banks,
To Germany we all sail'd o'er,
  To join the hostile ranks ;
At length in Ireland we arrived,
  After a long campaign,
Where a bonny maid my heart betrayed—
  She's Hibernia's lovely Jean.

Her cheeks were of the roseate hue,
  With the bright blinks of her e'en,
Besparkling with the drops of dew,
  That spangle the meadows green.
Jean Cameron ne'er was half so fair,
  No ! nor Jessy of Dumblane,
No princess fine can her outshine—
  She's Hibernia's lovely Jean.

This bonny lass of Irish braw,
  Was of a high degree,
Her parents said a soldier's bride
  Their daughter ne'er should be.

Overwhelmed with care, grief and despair,
  No hope does now remain,
Since the nymph divine cannot be mine,
  She's Hibernia's lovely Jean.

My tartan plaid I will forsake,
  My commission I'll resign,
I'll make this bonny lass my bride,
  If the lassie will be mine ;
Then in Ireland where the graces dwell,
  For ever I'll remain,
And in Hyman's band join heart in hand,
  Wi' Hibernia's lovely Jean.

Should war triumphant sound again,
  And call her sons to arms,
Or Neptune waft me o'er the flood,
  Far from Jeannie's charms ;
Should I be laid in honor's bed,
  By a ball or dart be slain,
Death's pangs would cure the pains I bear
  For Hibernia's lovely Jean.

Up for the Green.

[A song of the United Irishmen, 1796.]

AIR---Wearing of the Green.

'Tis the green—oh ! the green is the color of the true,
And we'll back it 'gainst the orange, and we'll raise it
    o'er the blue !
For the color of old Ireland alone should here be seen—
'Tis the color of the martyr'd dead—our own immortal
    green.
  Then up for the green, boys, and up for the green !
  Oh ! 'tis down to the dust, and a shame to be seen ;
  But we've hands—oh ! we've hands, boys, full strong
      enough, I ween,
  To rescue and to raise again our own immortal green!

SONGS OF OLD IRELAND.

They may say they have power 'tis vain to oppose—
'Tis better to obey and live, than surely die as foes ;
But we scorn all their threats, boys, whatever they
     may mean ;
For we trust in God above us, and we dearly love the
     green.
   So, we'll up for the green, and we'll up for the green!
   Oh! to *die* is far better than be curst as we have been ;
   And we've hearts—oh! we've hearts, boys, full true
     enough, I ween,
   To rescue and to raise again our own immortal green!

They may swear, as they often did, our wretchedness
     to cure ;
But we'll never trust John Bull again, nor let his lies
     allure.
No, we won't—no, we won't, Bull, for now nor ever
     more !
For we've hopes on the ocean, and we've trust on the
     shore.
   Then up for the green, boys, and up for the green !
   Shout it back to the Sasanach, " We'll *never* sell the
     green ! "
   For our TONE is coming back, and with men enough,
     I ween,
   To rescue, and avenge us and our own immortal
     green.

Oh, remember the days when their reign we did dis-
     turb,
At Limerick and Thurles, Blackwater and Benburb ;
And ask this proud Saxon if our blows he did enjoy,
When we met him on the battle-field of France—at
     Fontenoy.
   Then we'll up for the green, boys, and up for the
     green !
   Oh, 'tis still in the dust, and a shame to be seen ;
   But we've hearts and we've hands, boys, full strong
     enough, I ween,
   To rescue and to raise again our own unsullied green!

Willy Reilly.

"Oh, rise up, Willy Reilly, and come along with me,
I mean for to go with you and leave this counterie,
To leave my father's dwelling-house, his houses and
    free land ; "
And away goes Willy Reilly and his dear Colleen Bawn.°

They go by hills and mountains, and by yon lonesome
    plain,
Through shady groves and valleys all dangers to refrain ;
But her father followed after with a well-arm'd band,
And taken was poor Reilly and his dear Colleen Bawn.

It's home then she was taken, and in her closet bound,
Poor Reilly all in Sligo jail lay on the stony ground,
'Till at the bar of justice before the Judge he'd stand,
For nothing but the stealing of his dear Colleen Bawn.

"Now, in the cold, cold iron, my hands and feet are
    bound,
I'm handcuffed like a murderer, and tied unto the
    ground,
But all the toil and slavery I'm willing for to stand,
Still hoping to be succored by my dear Colleen Bawn."

The jailor's son to Reilly goes, and thus to him did say,
"Oh! get up, Willy Reilly, you must appear this day,
For great Squire Foillard's anger you never can with-
    stand,
I'm afear'd† you'll suffer sorely for your dear Colleen
    Bawn."

Now Willy's drest from top to toe all in a suit of green,
His hair hangs o'er his shoulders most glorious to be
    seen ;
He's tall and straight and comely as any could be
    found,
He's fit for Foillard's daughter, was she heiresss to a
    crown.

    * Fair young girl.   † Afraid.

" This is the news, young Reilly, last night that I did
 hear,
The lady's oath will hang you, or else will set you
 clear ; "
" If that be so," says Reilly, " her pleasure I will
 stand,
Still hoping to be succored by my dear Colleen Bawn."

The Judge he said, "This lady being in her tender
 youth,
If Reilly has deluded her, she will declare the truth ; "
Then, like a moving beauty bright before him she did
 stand,
" You're welcome there my heart's delight and dear
 Colleen Bawn."

" Oh, gentlemen," Squire Foillard said, " with pity
 look on me,
This villain came amongst us to disgrace our family ;
And by his base contrivances this villainy was planned,
If I don't get satisfaction I'll quit this Irish land."

The lady with a tear began, and thus replied she—
"The fault is none of Reilly's, the blame lies all on me;
I forced him for to leave his place and come along with me,
I loved him out of measure, which wrought our destiny."

Out spoke the noble Fox,* at the table he stood by,
" Oh ! gentlemen, consider on this extremity ;
To hang a man for love is a murder you may see,
So spare the life of Reilly, let him leave this counterie."

" Good, my lord, he stole from her, her diamonds and
 her rings,
Gold watch and silver buckles, and many precious
 things,
Which cost me in bright guineas more than five hundred pounds—
I'll have the life of Reilly should I lose ten thousand
 pounds."

* The prisoner's counsel.

"Good, my lord, I gave them him as tokens of true
          love,
And when we are a-parting I will them all remove,
If you have got them, Reilly, pray send them home to
          me."
"I will, my loving lady, with many thanks to thee."

"There is a ring among them I allow yourself to wear,
With thirty locket diamonds well set in silver fair,
And as a true-love-token wear it on your right hand,
That you'll think on my poor broken heart when you're
          in a foreign land."

Then out spoke noble Fox, "you may let the prisoner go,
The lady's oath has cleared him, as the jury all may
          know;
She has released her own true love, she has renewed his
          name,
May her honor bright gain high estate, and her offspring
          rise to fame!"

Colleen Bawn.

'Twas on a bright morning in summer
    I first heard his voice spakin' low,
As he said to a colleen beside me,
    Who's that purty girl milking her cow?
Oh! many times afther ye met me,
    An' vowed that I always should be
Your darlin' a cushla, alanna mavourneen,
    A suilish machree.

I havn't the manners or graces
    Of the girls in the world where ye move,
I havn't their beautiful faces,
    But oh! I've a heart that can love;
If it plaise ye, I'll dress me in satin,
    An' jewels I'll put on my brow,
But oh! don't be afther forgettin'
    Your purty girl milking her cow.

Molly, Asthore.

As down by Banna's banks I strayed, one evening in
    May,
The little birds in blythest notes made vocal every spray,
They sung their little notes of love, they sung them
    o'er and o'er—
Ah! gramachree, my colleen oge, my Molly, Asthore.

The daisy pied and all the sweets the dawn of Nature
    yields,
The primrose pale, the violet blue, lay scattered o'er
    the fields,
Such fragrance in the bosom lies of her whom I adore,
Ah! gramachree, my colleen oge, my Molly, Asthore.

I laid me down upon a bank, bewailing my sad fate,
That doomed me thus a slave to love, and cruel Molly's
    hate ;
How can she break the honest heart that wears her in
    its core,
Ah! gramachree, my colleen oge, my Molly, Asthore.

You said you loved me, Molly, dear—ah! why did I be-
    lieve ?
Yet who could think such tender words were meant but
    to deceive,
That love was all I asked on earth—nay! heaven could
    give no more.
Ah! gramachree, my colleen oge, my Molly, Asthore.

Oh! had I all the flocks that graze on yonder yellow
    hill,
Or lowed for me the numerous herds that yon green
    pasture fill,
With her I love I'd gladly share my kine and fleecy
    store,
Ah! gramachree, my colleen oge, my Molly, Asthore.

Two turtle-doves above my head, sat courting on a
bough,
I envied them their happiness to see them bill and coo,
Such fondness once for me was shown, but now, alas!
'tis o'er,
Ah! gramachree, my colleen oge, my Molly, Asthore.

Then fare thee well, my Molly dear, thy loss I e'er shall
mourn,
Whilst life remains in Stephen's neart 'twill beat for
thee alone,
Though thou art false, may heaven on thee its choicest
blessings pour,
Ah! gramachree, my colleen oge, my Molly, Asthore.

The Dear Irish Boy.

My Connor's cheeks are as ruddy as morn,
The brightest of pearls but mimic his teeth,
While nature with ringlets his mild brow adorn,
His hair's Cupid's bow-strings, and roses his breath.

CHORUS.

Smiling, beguiling, cheering, endearing,
Together oft o'er the mountain we've strayed,
By each other delighted, and fondly united,
I've listened all day to my dear Irish boy.

No roebuck more swifter can flee o'er the mountain,
No Briton bolder 'midst danger or scar ;
He's sightly, he's lightly, he's as clear as the fountain,
His eye's twinkling love, and he's gone to the war.
Smiling, &c.

The soft tuning lark it's notes shall cease to mourning,
The dull screaming owl shall cease its night sleep ;
While seeking lone walks in the shades of the evening,
If my Connor return not, I'll ne'er cease to weep.
Smiling, &c.

The war is all over, and my love is not returning ;
I fear that some envious plot has been laid,
Or some cruel goddess has him captivated ;
And left me to mourn here, a dear Irish maid.
   Smiling, &c.

Terence's Farewell to Kathleen.

So, my Kathleen, you're going to leave me,
 All alone by myself in this place;
But I'm sure you will never deceive me—
 Oh, no, if there is truth in that face.
Though England's a beautiful city,
 Full of illigant boys—oh, what then?
You wouldn't forget your poor Terence—
 You'll come back to old Ireland again!

It's a folly to keep you from going,
 Though, faith, it's a mighty hard case—
For, Kathleen, you know there's no knowing
 When next I shall see your sweet face.
And when you come back to me, Kathleen,
 None the better will I be off then;
You'll be speaking such beautiful English,
 Sure I won't know my Kathleen again.

Ah, now, where the need of this hurry?
 Don't flutter me so in this way;
I forgot, 'twixt grief and the flurry,
 Every word I was maning to say.
Now just wait a minute, I bid you—
 Can I talk, if you bother me so?
O Kathleen, my blessings go with you,
 E'ery inch of the way that you go!

Ma Allieen, Asthore.

When waking with the rosy day,
  From golden dreams of thee,
I watch the orient sunbeams play,
  Along the purple sea ;
Oh ! then I could not choose but weep,
  As thou were mine no more,
Ah ! gramachree, ma colleen oge,
  Ma Ailleen, Asthore !

When twilight brings the weeping hours,
  That sadden all the grove,
And angels leave their starry bowers
  To watch o'er faithful love,
Thy *parting words*, to me so sweet,
  I breath them o'er and o'er,
Ah ! gramachree, ma colleen oge,
  Ma Ailleen, Asthore !

But soon they'll lay me in the grave,
  Where broken hearts should be ;
And when, beyond the distant wave,
  Thou dream'st of meeting me,
My sorrows all will be forgot,
  And all the love I bore,
Ah ! gramachree, ma colleen oge,
  Ma Ailleen, Asthore !

The Lass o' Gowrie.

'Twas on a simmer's afternoon,
A wee before the sun gaed down,
My lassie wi' a braw new gown,
  Came o'er the hill to Gowrie.
The rosebud ting'd wi' morning show'rs,
Bloom'd fresh within the sunnie bow'rs,
But Kitty was the fairest flow'r,
  That ever bloom'd in Gowrie.

I had nae thought to do her wrang,
But round her waist my arms I flang,
And said my lassie will ye gang, ·
   To view the Carse o' Gowrie?
I'll take ye to my fathers ha',
In you green field beside the shaw
And make you lady o' them a',
   The brawest wife in Gowrie.

Soft kisses on her lips I laid,
The blush upon her cheek soon spread,
She whisper'd modestly, and said,
   "I'll gang wi' you to Gowrie."
The auld folk soon gi'ed their consent
And to Mess John we quickly went,
Who tied us to our hearts content,
   And now she's Lady Gowrie.

The Irish Jaunting Car.

My name is Larry Doolan, I'm a native of the soil,
If you want a day's diversion, I'll drive you out in
    style,
My car is painted red and green, and on the door a
    star,
And the pride of Dublin City is my Irish jaunting car.

CHORUS.

  Then, if you want to hire me, step into Mickey
    Mar's,
  And ask for Larry Doolan and his Irish jaunting
    cars.

When Queen Victoria came to Ireland her health to
    revive,
She asked the Lord Lieutenant to take her out to ride ;
She replied unto his greatness, before they traveled
    far,
How delightful was the jogging of the Irish jaunting
    car.

I'm hired by drunken men, tetotalers, and my friends,
But a carman has so much to do, his duty never ends ;
Night and day, both wet and dry, I travel near and
    far,
And at night I count the earnings of my Irish jaunting
    car.

Some say the Russian bear is tough, and I believe it's
    true,
Though we beat them at the Alma and Balaklava, too,
But if our Connaught Rangers would bring home the
    Russian Czar,
I would drive them off to blazes in my Irish jaunting
    car.

Some say all wars are over, I hope to God they are,
For you know full well they never were good for a
    jaunting car,
But peace and plenty—may they reign here, both near
    and far,
Then we'll drive to feasts and festivals in an Irish
    jaunting car.

They say they are in want of men, the French and Eng-
    lish, too,
And it's all about their commerce now they don't know
    what to do,
But if they come to Ireland our jolly sons to mar,
I'll drive them to the devil in my Irish jaunting car.

The Blarney.

Air---Kate Kearney.

Oh ! did you ne'r hear of the Blarney,
That's found near the banks of Killarney ?
        Believe it from me,
        No girls heart is free,
Once she hears the sweet sound of the Blarney.

For the Blarney's so great a desaiver,
That a girl thinks your there—tho' you leave her,
   And never finds out
   All the tricks you're about,
Till she's quite gone herself, with your Blarney.

Oh ! say, would you find this same Blarney,
There's a castle, not far from Killarney,
   On the top of the wall—
   But take care you don't fall,
There's a stone that contains all this Blarney.

Like a magnet, its influence such is,
That attraction it gives all it touches,
   If you kiss it, they say,
   That from that blessed day,
You may kiss whom you plaze, with your Blarney.

Green Grow the Rushes, O!

There's naught but care on every han',
   In every hour that passes, O!
What signifies the life o' man,
   An' 'twere na for the lasses, O?
      Green grow the rushes, O!
      Green grow the rushes, O!
      The sweetest hours that e'er I spent
      Are spent among the lasses, O!

The warly race may riches chase,
   An' riches still may fly them, O!
An' tho' at last they catch them fast,
   Their hearts can ne'er enjoy them, O!
      Green grow the rushes, &c.

Give me a cannie hour at e'en,
   My arms about my dearie, O!
Then warly cares and warly men
   May a' gae tapsalteerie, O!
      Green grow the rushes, &c.

For you sae douse ! ye sneer at this,
  Ye'er naught but senseless asses, O !
The wisest man the warl' e'er saw,
  He dearly loved the lasses, O !
    Green grow the rushes, &c.

Auld nature swears, the lovely dears
  Her noblest work she classes, O !
Her 'prentice han' she tried on man,
  And then she made the lasses, O !
    Green grow the rushes, &c.

Sergeant McFadgin.

[By permission of THOMAS DUNN ENGLISH, Esq.]

AIR—The Flaming O'Flennigans.

Whin I was a nate little bit of posterity,
  Runnin' about with my head full of fun,
Some one exclaimed with a touch of austerity —
  " Who in the devil's that son of a gun ? "
He saw there was fight in my eye, the rapscallion !
  Picking me out from the other gossoons ;
And that one day I'd be with my talents set value on,
  Orderly sergeant of Heavy Dragoons.
    Och ! gay is the life of a fighting Amerykin,
      Having no atin' to pay for, nor rint ;
    In battle, he rides to the fight like a harrykin,
      And when it's over sits down in his tint.

When grown, I got married, and that's an apprenticeship
  Makes a man master of war anyway ;
I soon left my colors, and fortune it sent a ship
  All for to carry me over the say.
Five years I was here when they made me a citizen ;
  But wanting stripes to my owld pantaloons,
And having ambition, which wasn't a bit of sin,
  Listed, I did, in the Heavy Dragoons.
    Och ! gay is the life, &c.

Talk of your Saizars, Napoleons and Hannibals—
    Galyant commanders of fame and renown—
Av they were fightin' with Brigham Young's Cannibals,
    Wouldn't the pride of their glory come down ?
Bellony herself, who of fightin' the goddess is,
    Not being up to the tricks of the coons,
Laving the haroes of Iliads and Odysseys,
    Has to depind on the Heavy Dragoons.
          Och ! gay is the life, &c.

Now I am out where of grass is no scarcity,
    But there's a plentiful lacking of trees ;
And I obsarve to my friends in adversity,
    Carry light hearts and be lively as fleas,
As for you Mormons, here comes Uncle Samuel,
    Marching his men to the livliest tunes ;
Sure every sowjer is ready to lam you well—
    Led to the fight by the Heavy Dragoons.
          Och ! gay is the life, &c.

Barnaby Finegan.

I'm a decent gay laboring youth,
    I was reared in the town of Dunshaughlin,
I'm a widower now in Maynooth,
    Since I buried sweet Molly M'Loughlin ;
I married but once in my life,
    But I'll never commit such a sin again ;
I discovered when she was my wife,
    She was fond of one Barnaby Finegan.

His father had cabins of mud
    That I often went to admire—
They were built at the time of the flood,
    To keep all his ancestors drier.
When he found I had Molly bespoke,
    He was getting quite fat, but got thin again,
In the struggle his gizzard he broke,
    And we'd a stiff of Poor Barnaby Finegan.

His corpse for convenience was put
   Among all his friends in the barn, sir,
Some traveled there upon foot,
   While others came mounted on garrons, sir ;
My wife for his loss cried and sobbed,
   Though I put her out twice she got in again,
But I gave her a boult in the gob,
   For which I was soon attacked by the Finegans.

The bed and the corpse was upset—
   The fighting commenced in a minute, sure,
Devil a stick could they get,
   Till they broke all the legs of the furniture.
In showers the blood flew about,
   Eyes were knocked out and shoved in again,
But I got a sowestering clout,
   That spilled me a top of poor Finegan.

How long I was dead I don't know—
   I couldn't believe I was living, sir—
I roused with the pain in my toes,
   For they had them both tied with a ribbon, sir ;
I opened my mouth for to speak,
   But the sheets was put up to my chin again ;
Molly roars out, "you know you're awake,
   You'll be tried with Barnaby Finegan."

"You lump of deception," I cried—
   And I thought to bounce up to knock her about,
By course as my two toes were tied,
   I was as fast as a spoon in thick stirabout ;
I soon got the use of my toes,
   By a friend of the corpse, Larry Gilligan,
He helped me to leap into clothes,
   To go spread a grass quilt over Finegan.

My she devil came on the spree,
   Full of whisky and grief from the berrin',
She showed as much mercy to me,
   As a hungry man shows to a herring ;

But one belly-go-fister I gave
  Her, that caused her to cry and to grin again,
In three months I opened the grave,
  And threw her on the bones with poor Finegan.

Now that I'm single again,
  I spend my time raking and battering,
I go to the fair with the men,
  And I dance with the maids at the patthern,
Then they think I am stuck to a T—
  They'll get shy, drop the talk, and begin again,
But they shan't come the huckle at me,
  For they might be acquainted with Finegan.

I'm not Myself at All.

Oh! I am not myself at all, Molly dear, Molly dear,
  I am not myself at all,
Nothing caring, nothing knowing, tis after you I'm going
Faith your shadow tis I'm growing, Molly dear, Molly
    dear,
  And I'm not myself at all.
Th' other day I went confessin', and I asked the fath-
    er's blessin'
  'But says I, "don't give me one entirely,
    For I fretted so last year, but the half o' me is here,
So give the other half to Molly Brierly;
  Oh! I'm not myself at all."

Oh! I'm not myself at all, Molly dear, Molly dear,
  My appetite's so small,
I once could pick a goose, but my buttons is no use,
Faith my tightest coat is loose, Molly dear, Molly dear,
  And I'm not myself at all.
If thus it is I waste, you'd better, dear, make haste,
  Before your lover's gone away entirely,
    If you don't soon change your mind,
    Not a bit o' me you'll find,
And what 'ud you think o' that, Molly Brierly?
  Oh! I'm not myself at all.

Oh ! my shadow on the wall, Molly dear, Molly dear,
   Is'nt like myself at all.
For I've got so very thin, myself says 'tis'nt him,
But that purty girl so slim, Molly dear, Molly dear,
   And I'm not myself at all.
If thus I smaller grow, all fretting, dear, for you,
  'Tis you should make me up the deficiency,
    So just let Father Taaf
    Make you my better half,
And you will not the worse for the addition be ;
   Oh ! I'm not myself at all.

I'll be not myself at all, Molly dear, Molly dear,
   'Till you my own I call ;
Since a change o'er me there came, sure you might
   change your name,
And 'twould just come to the same, Molly dear, Molly
   dear,
   Oh ! 'twould just come to the same ;
For if you and I were one, all confusion would be gone,
  And 'twould simplify the mather entirely,
    And 'twould save us so much bother,
    When we'd both be one another,
So listen now to rayson Molly Brierly;
   Oh ! I'm not myself at all.

Darling Old Stick.

My name is Morgan McCarthy, from Trim !
My relations are all dead except one, brother Jim—
  And he's now gone soulgering to Cape Hull,
  And I expect he's laid low with a nick in his skull!

CHORUS :

   Let him be dead or alivin',
   A prayer for his soul shall be given,
   That he shall be sent home or to heaven,
For he left me this Darling Old Stick !

If this stick it could spake, it would tell you some tales,
And batter the countenances of the O'Nales !
  It has caused bits o' skull to fly up in the air ;
  It was the promotion of fun at every fair.
The last time I used it 'twas on Patrick's Day,
Larry Fagan and I jumped into a shay ;
  We went to a fair at the side of Athloy,
  Where we danced, and when done, kissed Kate Mc-
    Alvoy !
    And her sweetheart went out for her cousin ;
    By the powers he brought in a dozen.
    What a daldum they'd have knocked us in,
  If I hadn't 'ave had this Darling Old Stick !

War ! was the word when a faction came in.
For they pummeled me well—they stripped off to the
    skin !
  Like a rector I stood, watching the attack.
  And the first one came up I knocked on his back !
    Then I poked out the eye of Pat Glancy,
    For he once humbugged my sister Nancy !
    In the meantime Miss Kate took a fancy
  To me and my innocent Stick !

I smathered her sweetheart until he was black,
Kate tipped me the wink, we were off in a thwack !
  We went to a house at the end of the town,
  Where we kept up our spirits by pouring some down.
    When the whiskey began for to warm her,
    I got her snug up in a corner ;
    She said her sweetheart would inform on her !
  'Twas there I said praise to my Stick !

Kate she drank whiskey to such a degree
That for her support she had to lean upon me ;
  I said I would see her safe to her abode,
  'Twas there we fell in the middle of the road.
    Until roused by the magistrate's orders,
    Devil a toe could we go farther,
    Surrounded by police for murder,
  Was myself and my innocent Stick.

When I was acquitted I jumped from the dock,
An' all the gay fellows around me did flock,
　　They gave me a sore arm they shook my hand so often,
　　It was only for fear of seeing my own coffin !
　　　　I went and I bought a gold ring, sirs,
　　　　Miss Kate to the Priest I did bring, sirs—
　　　　That night we did joyfully sing, sirs,
　　The adventures of myself and my Stick !

Erin go Bragh.

Green were the fields where my forefathers dwelt,
Oh ! Erin, mavourneen, slan laght go bragh.
Tho' our farm it was small, yet comfort we felt,
Oh ! Erin, mavourneen, slan laght go bragh !
At length came the day when our lease did expire,
And fain would I live where before lived my sire,
But ah, well-a-day, I was forced to retire ;
Erin, mavourneen, slan laght go bragh.

Though all taxes I paid, yet no vote could I pass, oh !
Erin, mavourneen, slan laght go bragh !
Aggrandized no great man, and I felt it, alas ! oh !
Erin, mavourneen, slan laght go bragh !
Forced from my home, yea, where I was born,
To range the wide world, poor, helpless, forlorn ;
I look back with regret, and my heart-strings are torn,
Erin, mavourneen, slan laght go bragh !

With principles pure, patriotic, and firm,
Erin, mavourneen, slan laght go bragh !
Attach'd to my country, a friend to reform,
Erin, mavourneen, slan laght go bragh !
I supported old Ireland, was ready to die for it,
If her foes e'er prevailed, I was well known to sigh
　　　for it ;
By my faith I preserved, and am now forced to fly
　　　for it :
Erin, mavourneen, slan laght go bragh !

He Tells me He Loves Me.

He tells me he loves me, and can I believe,
The heart he has won he would wish to deceive;
For ever and always his sweet words to me
Are aileen, mavorneen, a cushla macree.

Last night when we parted, his gentle good-bye,
A thousand times said, and each time with a sigh ;
And still the same sweet words he whispers to me,
My aileen, mavourneen, a cushla macree.

The friend of my childhood, the hope of my youth,
Whose heart is all pure, whose words are all truth ;
Oh! still the same words he whispers to me
Are aileen, mavourneen, a cushla macree.

Oh! when will the day come, the dear happy day,
That a maiden may hear all a lover can say,
And he speaks out the words he now whispers to me,
My aileen, mavourneen, a cushla macree.

Limerick Races.

I'm a simple Irish lad, I've resolved to see some fun,
    sirs,
  So, to satisfy my mind, to Limerick town I come, sirs;
Oh, murther! what a precious place, and what a charm-
    ing city,
  Where the boys are all so free, and the girls are all
    so pretty.
        Musha ring a ding a da,
        Ri too ral laddy Oh !
        Musha ring a ding a da,
        Ri too ral laddy Oh !

It was on the first of May, when I began my rambles,
  When everything was there, both jaunting cars and
    gambols ;

I looked along the road, what was lined with smiling
      faces,
   All driving off, ding-dong, to go and see the races.
            Musha ring a ding a da, &c.

So then I was resolved to go and see the race, sirs,
   And on a coach and four I neatly took my place, sirs,
When a chap bawls out, "behind!" and the coachman
      dealt a blow, sirs —
   Faith, he hit me just as fair as if his eyes were in his
      poll, sirs.
            Musha ring a ding a da, &c.

So then I had to walk, and make no great delay, sirs,
   Until I reached the course, where everything was
      gay, sirs ;
It's then I spied a wooden house, and in the upper
      story,
   The band struck up a tune, called "Garry Owen and
      glory."
            Musha ring a ding a da, &c.

There was fiddlers playing jigs, there was lads and
      lasses dancing,
   And chaps upon their nags, round the course sure
      they were prancing,
Some was drinking whisky-punch, while others bawl'd
      out gaily,
   "Hurrah then for the shamrock green, and the
      splinter of shillelagh.
            Musha ring a ding a da, &c.

There was betters to and fro, to see who would win the
      race, sirs,
   And one of the sporting chaps of course came up to
      me, sirs ;
Says he, "I'll bet you fifty pounds, and I'll put it down
      this minute."
   "Ah, then, ten to one," says I, "the foremost horse
      will win it."
            Musha ring a ding a da, &c.

When the players came to town, and a funny set was
    they,
 I paid my two thirteens to go and see the play,
They acted kings and cobblers, queens, and everything
    so gaily,
  But I found myself at home when they struck up
    " Paddy Carey."
        Musha ring a ding a da, &c.

Teddy O'Neal.

I've come to the cabin he danced his wild jigs in,
As neat a mud palace as ever was seen ;
And, consid'ring it served to keep poultry and pigs in,
I'm sure it was always most elegant clean.
But now all about it seems lonely and dreary,
All sad and all silent, no piper, no reel ;
Not even the sun, through the casement, is cheery,
Since I miss the dear darling boy, Teddy O'Neale.

I dreamt but last night—oh ! bad luck to my dreaming,
I'd die if I thought 'twould come truly to pass—
But I dreamt, while tears down my pillow were
    streaming,
That Teddy was courting another fair lass ;
Oh ! didn't I wake with a weeping and wailing,
The grief of that thought was too deep to conceal ;
My mother cried—" Norah, child, what is your ailing?"
And all I could utter was—"Teddy O'Neale."

Shall I never forget when the big ship was ready,
And the moment was come when my love must depart ;
How I sobb'd, like a spalpeen, " Good bye to you
    Teddy,"
With drops on my cheek and a stone at my heart.
He says 'tis to better his fortune he's roving,
But what would be gold to the joy I should feel
If I saw him come back to me, honest and loving,
Still poor, but my own darling, Teddy O'Neale.

Widow Machree.

Widow machree, 'tis no wonder you frown,
   Och hone ! widow machree,
Faith it ruins your looks that same dirty black gown,
   Och hone ! widow machree.
 How altered your air,
 With that close cap you wear,
 'Tis destroying your hair,
   That should be flowing free;
 Be no longer a churl
 Of its black silken curl,
   Och hone ! widow machree.

Widow machree ! now the summer is come,
   Och hone ! widow machree.
When everything smiles, should a beauty look glum,
   Och hone ! widow machree.
 See the birds go in pairs,
 And the rabbits and hares,
 Why even the bears
   In couples agree,
 And the mute little fish,
 Though they can't spake, they wish,
   Och hone ! widow machree.

Widow machree, and when winter comes in,
   Och hone ! widow machree,
To be poking the fire all alone is a sin,
   Och hone ! widow machree.
 Why, the shovel and tongs
 To each other belongs,
 And the kettle sings songs
   Full of family glee ;
 While alone with your cup,
 Like a hermit you sup,
   Och hone ! widow machree.

And how do you know, with the comforts I've towld,
   Och hone ! widow machree.
But you're keeping some poor fellow out in the cowld,
   Och hone ! widow machree.

With such sins on your head,
Sure your peace would be fled—
Could you sleep on your bed,
       Without thinking to see
Some ghost or some sprite,
That would wake you each night,
       Crying, och hone! widow machree.

Then take my advice, darling widow machree,
       Och hone! widow machree,
And with my advice, faith, I wish you'd take me,
       Och hone! widow machree.
You'd have me to desire,
And to stir up the fire,
And, sure, hope is no liar,
       In whispering to me,
That the ghosts would depart
When you'd be near my heart,
       Och hone! widow machree.

A Sweet Irish Girl is the Darling.

If they talk about ladies, I'll tell the plan
Of myself—to be sure I'm a nate Irishman,
There is neither sultana nor foreign ma'mselle
That has charms to please me, or can coax me so well
As the sweet Irish girl, so charming to see:
Och! a tight Irish girl is the darling for me.
And sing lillilloo, fire away, frisky she'll be;
Och! a sweet Irish girl is the darling for me.
     For she's pretty, she's witty,
     She's hoaxing, and coaxing,
     She's smiling, beguiling to see, to see:
     She rattles, she prattles,
     She dances, and prances,
Och! a sweet Irish girl is the darling for me.

Now, some girls they are little, and some they are
    tall,
Och! others are big, sure, and others are small ;
And some that are teazing, are bandy, I tell ;
Still none can please me, or can coax me so well
As the dear Irish girl, so charming to see ;
Och! a sweet Irish girl is the darling for me.
        For she's pretty, &c.

The Land of Potatoes, O!

AIR—Morgan Rattler.

If I had on the clear
But five hundred a year,
"Tis myself would not fear
    Without adding a farthing to 't ;
Faith if such was my lot,
Little Ireland's the spot
Where I'd build a snug cot,
    With a bit of garden to 't.
As for Italy's dales,
With their Alps and high vales,
Where with fine squalling gales,
    Their signoras so treat us, O !
I'd ne'er to them come,
Nor abroad ever roam,
But enjoy a sweet home
    In the land of potatoes, O !
Hospitality, all reality, no formality,
        There you ever see ;
But free and easy 'twould so amaze ye, you'd think us
    all crazy,
        For dull we never be !

If my friend honest Jack,
Would but take a small hack,
And just get on his back,
    And with joy gallop full to us ;
He, throughout the whole year,
Then should have the best cheer,

For faith none so dear
  As our brother, John Bull, to us !
And we'd teach him, when there,
Both to blunder and swear,
And our brogue with him share,
  Which both genteel and neat is, O !
And we'd make him so drink,
By St. Patrick, I think,
That he never would shrink
  From the land of potatoes, O !
    Hospitality, &c.

Though I freely agree
I should more happy be
If some lovely she
  From Old England would favor me ;
For no spot on earth
Can more merit bring forth,
If with beauty and worth
  You embellish'd would have her be ;
Good breeding, good nature,
You find in each feature,
That nought you've to teach her—
  So sweet and complete she's, O !
Then if fate would but send
Unto me such a friend,
What a life would I spend
  In the land of potatoes, O !
    Hospitality, &c.

The Croppy Boy.

[A Ballad of '98.]

" Good men and true ! in this house who dwell,
To a stranger bouchal° I pray you tell
Is the priest at home ? or may he be seen ?
I would speak a word with Father Green."

° Boy.

" The priest's at home, boy, and may be seen ;
'Tis easy speaking with Father Green ;
But you must wait till I go and see
If the holy Father alone may be."

The youth has entered an empty hall—
What a lonely sound has his light foot-fall !
And the gloomy chamber's chill and bare,
With a vested priest in a lonely chair.

The youth has knelt to tell his sins ;
" *Nomine Dei*," the youth begins ;
At " *mea culpa*" he beats his breast,
And in broken murmurs he speaks the rest.

" At the siege of Ross did my father fall,
And at Gorey my loving brothers all.
I alone am left of my name and race ;
I will go to Wexford and take their place.

" I cursed three times since last Easter day—
At mass-time once I went to play ;
I passed the churchyard one day in haste,
And forgot to pray for my mother's rest.

" I bear no hate against living thing ;
But I love my country above my king.
Now, Father ! bless me, and let me go,
To die, if God has ordained it so."

The priest said nought, but a rustling noise
Made the youth look up in wild surprise ;
The robes were off, and in scarlet there
Sat a yoeman captain with fiery glare.

With fiery glare and with fury hoarse,
Instead of blessing, he breathed a curse :—
" 'Twas a good thought, boy, to come here and shrive,
For one short hour is your time to live.

At Geneva Barrack that young man died,
And at Passage they have his body laid.
Good people who live in peace and joy,
Give a prayer and a tear for the Croppy Boy.

THE
EMERALD SONGSTER.

PART II.

NOW CAN'T YOU BE AISY.

Mickey Free's Song. From "Charles O'Malley."
Air, "Arrah, Katty, now can't you be aisy."

Oh! what stories I'll tell when my sodgering's o'er,
  And the gallant fourteenth is disbanded;
Not a drill nor parade will I hear of no more,
  When safely in Ireland I'm landed.
With the blood that I spilt—the Frenchmen I kilt,
  I'll drive all the girls half crazy;
And some 'cute one will cry, with a wink of her eye,
  "Mr. Free, now—why can't you be aisy?"

I'll tell how we routed the squadrons in fight,
  And destroyed them all at "Talavera,"
And then I'll just add how we finished the night,
  In learning to dance the "Bolera;"
How by the moonshine we drank raal wine,
  And rose next day fresh as a daisy;
Then some one will cry, with a look mighty sly,
  "Arrah, Mickey—now can't you be aisy?"

I'll tell how the nights with Sir Arthur we spent,
  Around a big fire in the air too,
Or may be enjoying ourselves in a tent,
  Exactly like Donnybrook fair too;
How he'd call out to me—"pass the wine, Mr. Free,
  For you're a man never is lazy!"
Then some one will cry, with a wink of her eye,
  "Arrah, Mickey dear—can't you be aisy?"
  1*

I'll tell, too, the long years in fighting we passed,
  Till Mounseer asked Bony to lead him;
And Sir Arthur, grown tired of glory at last,
  Begged of one Mickey Free to succeed him.
But, "acushla," says I, "the truth is, I'm shy!
  There's a lady in Ballynacrazy!
And I swore on the book—" she gave me a look,
  And cried, "Mickey—now can't you be aisy?"

OH! ONCE WE WERE ILLIGANT PEOPLE.

From "Charles O'Malley."

Oh! once we were illigant people,
  Though we now live in cabins of mud;
And the land that ye see from the steeple
  Belonged to us all from the flood.
My father was then king of Connaught,
  My grandaunt viceroy of Tralee;
But the Sassenach came, and signs on it!
  The divil an acre have we.

The least of us then were all earls,
  And jewels we wore without name!
We drank punch out of rubies and pearls—
  Mr. Petrie can tell you the same.
But, except some turf mould and potatoes,
  There's nothing our own we can call:
And the English—bad luck to them!—hate us,
  Because we've more fun than them all!

My grandaunt was niece to St. Kevin,
  That's the reason my name's Mickey Free!
Priest's nieces—but sure he's in Heaven,
  And his failins is nothin' to me.
And we still might get on without doctors,
  If they'd let the ould island alone;
And if purplemen, priests, and tithe-proctors
  Were crammed down the great gun of Athlone.

KILL OR CURE.

Written and Composed by J. H. Ogden.

I'M a roving Irish boy, I was born in Dallaraghan,
And christen'd with much joy after my father Patrick
    Faghan ;
I had a sweet-heart Katty, and I courted her so gaily,
Divil a thought had I of trouble as I twisted my shillelah.
Musha Katty O'Shaughnessy, she's the girl for me,
Whack fal the daddy, musha Katty O'Shaughnessy.

Och ! 'Twas herself I courted, a girl both nate and cosey,
She said she loved me in return, her cheeks were round
    and rosy,
Of sov'reigns I had twinty, and says she I've siventeen.
Faith we'll join ourselves and them together, and live like
    king and queen.
Musha Katty O'Shaughnessy, she's the girl for me,
Whack fal the daddy, musha Katty O'Shaughnessy.

So we both set sail for Liverpool and pack'd our kits to-
    gether,
And married got so nate and cool in spite of wind and
    weather ;
With our money we open'd a shop in a business not
    amiss,
We sold oysters, haddocks, mac'rel, mussels, praties and
    fry'd fish.
Musha Katty O'Shaughnessy, she's the girl for me,
Whack fal the daddy, musha Katty O'Shaughnessy.

In business we did well, till one day she was taken ill, sir.
And the doctor almost ruin'd me with sending in his bill,
    sir,
So I made a bargain with him "*kill or cure*" for twenty
    pounds, so frisky,
He was a decent sort so I thought I'd stand a naggin of
    whiskey.
Musha Katty O'Shaughnessy, she is the girl for me,
Whack fal the daddy, musha Katty O'Shaughnessy.

But she grew worse and worse, which made me quake with
  fear, sir,
The doctor he attended her for more than half a year,
  sir.
Till one fine morn she died, and myself it did bewilder,
And the doctor wanted his twenty pounds (*Spoken*) says I
  you never cur'd her?
No says he, then says I (*singing*) you dar not say you
  kill'd her!
Musha Katty O'Shaughnessy, she was the girl for me,
Whack fal the daddy, Musha Katty O'Shaughnessy.

So gintlemen injoy yourselves, the whiskey drink like
  thunder.
Yez cannot help but own yourselves there's mirth in an
  Irish blunder,
But when for your wives a doctor yez want, mind and yez
  be sure,
Make the bargain like I did myself with the doctor "*kill
  or cure!*"
Musha Katty O'Shaughnessy, that's the style for me,
Whack fal the daddy, musha Katty O'Shaughnessy.

THE SNOB AND THE TAILOR.

Recitation.   (Given with great applause, by J. H. Ogden.)

Twas in ould Ireland, in Dublin's famed city,
Where the girls are all fair, and the boys all witty,
There were a snob and a tailor lived next-door neighbors,
And they did very well by the fruits of their labors.
The snob had once been a stout grenadier,
And served in the army for many a long year;
He had gained a pension, for good reason why,
Because he'd blinked at his foes till he'd lost one eye.
He'd lost part of his nose, which was a worse job,
For the boys used to call him, "Ould Nosey, the snob."
Now, the tailor used to wear a hump on his back,
And the boys in the street used to call it his "son Jack."

He was little, decrepit, and besides the big hump,
One leg was made like the arm of a pump;
And he often would swear, by the mortal St. Mike,
He'd long for the day when he could shoulder his pike.
Says he, "I'd skiver the red coats, friends, brothers, and
    cousins.
And have them hung up to dry like red herrings by
    dozens,
For who would not fight to set Ireland free,
And stand by O'Connell, and sweet liberty!"
Now, it was at the sign of the Pig and Shilalagh
Where the snob and the tailor their battles fought daily;
But their weapons were satire, low and severe—
But you cannot expect pearls to drop out of a pig's ear.
"Now," says the tailor, "here's bad luck to every red coat,
That would for a shilling a-day turn cut throat;
And every raw lobster that ever wore the cloth;
I include you amongst them, old Bottle the Broth!"
Says the snob, "You dare not say that again;
You are not the man—you're a thing—
Fit for nothing; it's prate, sure, you can!
You may toss off your porter, and act your vagaries;
Why, you was changed in the nurse by the fairies!
Why, you little, decrepit, jew-looking *monsieur*,
You'd look well with your pike and jacket of green!
But come, Mr. Tailor, and tell me the truth,
How ould is a louse before it has a double tooth?"
And thus they went on in jaw every night;
'Twas all they could do, for it never came to a fight;
For the snob was a big fellow, clever and tall;
And the tailor was little, decrepit, and small.
It was pride that kept the snob from resorting to blows,
And it was fear that let the little man's valor repose.
Now it happened one morning, both of them went out;
Each, of course, took his own way, with his pipe near his
    snout;
Till, by chance, they met on the banks of the Liffy,
When each armed his jaws for war in a jiffy.
"Good morning," says the snob, "you are loaded just
    early—

I'm sure before night you'll be tired out fairly:
Before that big hump on my back I would trudge it.
On my soul, I'd sooner carry a stout tinker's budget."
That was a hard slap for poor snip; but when he though:
    on snob's eye,
There was wit came in aid to the tailor's reply.
Says the tailor, "It's rather early with you, for, by the
    same token,
You have only got one of your window shutters open;
And when you open both your shutters, friend Jack,
I then will remove this large hump off my back."

THE IRISHMAN.

With an additional verse by J. H. Ogden.—AIR, "The Englishman."

'Tis myself that bears an illigant name,
    And who dare say it is not?
I was born one day when my mother was out,
    In a nate little mud-built cot.
My father was the broth of a boy,
    And my mother was the same,—
The reason, my jewels, do you hear,
    That I bear such an illigant name.

CHORUS:

I'm the broth of a boy, deny it who can,
And my mother's a true-born Irishman!
I'm the broth of a boy, deny it who can,
And my mother's a true-born Irishwoman!

There's the English, the Irish, the Scotch, and the Welcl
    And success to them all jolly four;
And bad luck to me if one of them will flinch,
    If there was but one to a score.
For John Bull's cold steel will make them freeze;
    Paddy's shillelah will warm them enough;
Taffy will choke them with red-hot toasted cheese;
    And Scotchey will blind them with snuff.

CHORUS:

'Tis a glorious army, deny it who can,
John Bull, Taffy, Scotchey, and an Irishman
'Tis a glorious army, deny it who can,
John Bull, Taffy, Scotchey, and an Irishman!

At the city of Delhi we gave them cayanne,
And our sojers they fought first-rate;
And with determination went in every man,
When they blew up the Cashmere gate.
The word of command from our Generals did fly,
And lion-hearted fought officers and men,
Blood for blood, was our country's cry,
And we'll never trust the Indians again!

CHORUS:

For our country can conquer by land or sea;
On, boys, for death or victory!
On, brave army! on, my boys!
One Irishman can lick ten Sepoys!

PAT'S CURIOSITY SHOP.

A New Comic Song.

You'VE heard talk of Paddy's museum,
Its modern and ancient antiques,
If not, when you listen you'll hear 'em,
Of their fame all ould Ireland speaks.
I was ever looked on as a lover
Of ancient antiques from my birth,
So I thought I'd a right to discover,
What nobody else could on earth.

CHORUS:

Oh, a fig for your Barnum's Museum,
When you can, at my house you may stop,
You'll be split like a stone when you see 'em,
At Pat's curiosity shop.

I've bolted ten times through the globe, sir,
  To bring all my wonders away;
I have borrowed the patience of Job, sir,
  To keep me awake night and day;
With politeness, oh ain't I been treated,
  Never kilt—though thrice cut in two—
But you'll stare at me when I've repeated,
  My string of antiquities through.

Oh, a fig, &c.

I've two, more than all I take pride in,
  One's old mother Shipton's birch broom,
On which the old *gal* would fly striding—
  And the watch of the man of the moon.
I've a frozen flame from Mount Etna,
  Caught by a man passing by:
A sly Cupid's dart forged at Gretna,
  With the lash of Pope Gregory's eye.

Oh, a fig, &c

I've got a full grown alligator,
  That in sleep turned himself inside out;
The tail of the great Agitator,
  With a knot of the first Russian Knout.
I've a pair of kid shoes made of satin,
  A nutmeg as big as your head;
The chair that old King Canute sat in,
  And a cobweb as heavy as lead.

Oh, a fig, &c.

I've a walking stick thick as my arm,
  That belonged to O'Brien, the brave,
I've got mother Hubbard's great charm,
  Drowned sailors from shipwreck to save,
I've the bustle of Jupiter's mother,
  With Mercury's grandmother's stays;
And I've got the steel pen of my brother,
  With which he wrote all Shakspeare's plays.

Oh, a fig, &c.

I've got Dr. Bushby's old table,
  The cap of Bill Somers the fool,
The roof of the tower of Babel,
  With prince Donohoe's three-legged stool.
I've a beetle as big as a bowl,
  That would hold twenty gallons or more,
And the very identical roll
  The baker gave Mrs. Jane Shore.
            Oh, a fig, &c.

I've the snout of old Whittington's cat,
  Patched coats without any stitches;
Adam's spade, and his four-and-nine hat,
  With a pair of King William's breeches.
I've got the snuff-box of Mahomet,
  An Irish nobleman's wig;
And Miss Queen Elizabeth's bonnet,
  And the brain of the famed learned pig.
            Oh, a fig, &c.

I've the bone of the shoulder of mutton,
  That was roasted at Anthony's feast,
And a beautiful pearly white button,
  Off the coat of an old Druid priest.
I've got, too, the harp of Timotheus,
  That played Alexander to sleep,
The poker with which he killed Clytus,
  Which caused all the country to weep.
            Oh, a fig, &c.

I've got his great horse's tail too,
  Domitian's long baccy pipe,
Cleopatra's purple silk sail too,
  And a bee twice the size of a snipe.
I could tell—but the doctors declare
  More singing would soon turn my brain,
But some other time I don't care,
  When you drop in, to sing 'em again.
            Oh, a fig, &c.

PADDY CONNER.

As sung by J. H. Ogden.—Arr, Judy Kalligan.

'TWAS on last Sunday morn, the news to me was carried,
That Paddy and Judy Conner had trotted away to be
    married;
I saddled my donkey quick, I gave him such a whack, sir,
With my shillelah stick, I was after them in a crack, sir.

CHORUS:

Och! what joy, nothing we was dreading,
Roaring boys, at Paddy Conner's wedding.

Then we gallop'd away, till we came to Mother Miles's
And there I heard them say they were gone up to Saint
    Giles's;
I flew there in a trice, and there was such a rout, sir,
Together they were spliced, and all came tumbling out, sir.
                  Och! what joy, &c.

Then we went away to Judy Conner's mother,
And into the door we rolled on top of one another;
There was Larry, Kate, and Peg, and about a dozen more,
And Conner with his leg he broke the cupboard door.
                  Och! what joy, &c

There we sat on the ground drinking altogether,
The whiskey it went round, our hearts as light as fea-
    thers;
We had rum, beer, ale, and toast, and butter to put on the
    crumpets,
And a little pig to roast, the women all to comfort.
                  Och! what joy, &c.

The supper it was done, 'twas break of day in the morn-
    ing,
We swore we'd have some fun, all fear and danger scorn-
    ing;
I went and hit Conner a blow because he struck my mo-
    ther,

And all at once, you know we were wallopping one
    another.
                         Och! what joy, &c.

Just like a lump of lead, we both came tumbling down,
    sir,
And against the bedstead leg, I cracked his collar bone,
    sir;
Then Connor, out of spite, to please his own desire,
Went out and got a light, and set the place on fire.
                         Och! what joy, &c.

And then they went away frightened out of breath.
The goods and every feather and all was burnt to death;
Then I went away, the divil a word I said,
I saw no more of the fun, but tumbled into bed.
                         Och! what joy, &c.

THE REAL IRISH STEW.

With an additional verse by J. H. Ogden.—Air, Red, White and Blue.

Some like herrings red from the ocean,
    And others like a lump of pig's fry;
Some like pig's cheek, I've a notion,
    Others dine off puddings and pies;
In the cook shops there's thousands assemble,
    And they relish stew made out of glue,
But to me there's nothing can resemble
    A blow out of real Irish stew.
        Three cheers for some real Irish stew,
        Three cheers for some real Irish stew,
        And to me there's nothing can resemble
        A blow out of real Irish stew.

When the potato blight spread desolation,
    And threatened our land to deform,
Old Nicholas insulted our nation,
    But he never got over the storm;

For our soldiers and sailors were ready,
And to the devil his granite walls they blew,
And the fact that kept our Britons steady,
Was having their ribs lined with stew.
Three cheers for some real Irish stew, &c.

At Alma, Inkerman, and Sebastopol,
Our troops they fought like men,
And Raglan sent despatches to England
That for our noble queen they'd do the same again;
Then the English and the French they assaulted,
And the Russians from the Malakoff they flew,
And the banner of our allies was planted,
And each man had a barrel full of stew.
Three cheers for some real Irish stew, &c.

Then the stew, boys, the stew, boys, bring hither,
And we'll sup it till we're full up to the brim,
May the stew of St. Patrick never wither,
Nor the name of old Murphy grow dim;
May the onions and the spuds never sever,
Whilst there's good country beef brought in view,
Here's our army out in India for ever,
And three cheers for an Irish stew,
Three cheers for an Irish stew, &c.

THE LAND OF OULD ERIN.

Sung by J. H. Ogden.

THE land of ould Erin's the land of delight,
Where the women can love, and the men can all fight;
We have hearts for the girls, and arms for our foes,
And they both are triumphant, so all the world knows.
You may talk of politeness—we beat them at that,
For when the Frenchman came courting, a rival of Pat,
Says he, my dear jewel, you're quite at a stand,
So take hold of my foot, it will lend you a hand,

So let us be frisky, and tipple the whiskey,
Long life to ould Erin and liberty's joys;
No country whatever hath power to sever
The shamrock, the rose, and the thistle, my boys.

They may talk of their living, it's blarney and stuff,
For when a man's hungry he can eat fast enough,
As for teaching a live man to live, it's my eye,
Let him go over to Ireland and they'll teach him to die;
Their frogs and soup maigre, it's nothing but froth,
When compared with our praties and Scotch barley broth,
What land like ould Erin for living so fit,
Hospitality's home, and the birth-place of wit.
                    So let us be frisky, &c.

They may talk of their wonders as long as they please,
By St. Patrick, their swans are nothing but geese;
They talk about fighting, it's all they can say,
For as soon as we charg'd they all ran away.
Then long life to our land, that grows out of the sea,
May it flourish in prosperity, happy and free;
For England and Ireland can prove,
That we beat them in courage, in beauty, and love.
                    So let us be frisky, &c.

THE IRISHMAN'S WAGER.

Sung by J. H. Ogden.

Two Paddies one day on a common had met, with some of
    their friends rough and hearty,
They challenged each other, and two made a bet, Paddy
    Rourke could'nt carry Macarthy,
By jabers, says Paddy, give your hand but I will, I'll carry
    him like a young donkey,
To the top of the ladder, if he will sit still, on the hod
    which they call my monkey.

CHORUS:
> Singing philliloo Pat, Paddy Neale, Paddy
> whack,
> Irish buttermilk, herrings, and whiskey,
> You divels, come eat, fight, and drink, till ye
> crack,
> By the powers St. Patrick was friskey.

Then they all marched in order, and bold Paddy Rourke
fetched his hod out in a minute,
And he shoulder'd Macarthy, who said, with a look at the
hod, "by the powers I'm in it;"
Then the people all round hail'd them both with a shout,
to the ladder as they were advancing;
Some cried to him, Paddy, mind and don't spill him out,
and others were laughing and dancing.
> Singing philliloo Pat, Paddy Neale, Paddy
> whack, &c.

At the end of the common new houses were built, and each
of them stood ten stories,
The women cried out, Macarthy 'll be kilt; but Macarthy in the hod was in glory,
When O'Rourke up the ladder a few steps had trod, Macarthy cried out "you will lose it;"
"Shall I," says Paddy, "I've holt of the hod, you're in
it, fall out if you choose it."
> Singing philliloo Pat, Paddy Neale, Paddy
> whack, &c.

Then Pat stepp'd it out till he came to the top, and there
for his friends was waiting,
They all took a bottle of whiskey up the ladder to stop
to have a day on the new slating;
When Pat got to the top the house it was crammed, and
they cheer'd him when he crossed it,
But Macarthy said, when half way up, "I'll be damn'd,
I was in good hopes Paddy Rourke would have
lost it."
> Singing philliloo Pat, Paddy Neale, Paddy
> whack, &c.

The houses were finish'd, and ten stories high, some drunk
    on the roof were strolling.
  The weight of the lot made the rafters to fly, and some
    down below were seen rolling;
Norah and Judy, and the rest of the squad, they fell into a
    cistern of water,
  And O'Rourke and Macarthy fell down in the hod, and
    were smothered completely in mortar.
            Singing philliloo Pat, Paddy Neale, Paddy
            whack, &c.

PADDY'S WAKE.

Sung by J. H. Ogden.—AIR, Bay of Biscay.

Loud bawl'd each Irish mourner that went to Paddy's
    wake,
The house in every corner began to twist and shake;
To view Paddy in his shroud
The neighbors all did crowd,
'Mid shouts and cries that reached the skies,
Paddy, what the devil made yez die, och hone!

Then the house began to shiver, and the stacks of chim-
    neys bent,
And the rain, like a thundering big river, through every
    tile-hole went;
Then they sat down upon the floor,
And Paddy was placed before;
And each one did mourn, Paddy you're dead and gone,
What the devil made yez die, och hone!

Then the time it came for starting to lay Paddy in his grave,
And each took a great big parting, and Peter sang a
    beautiful stave;
Then they screwed Paddy down in his shell,
And gave him tobacco and snuff as well,
And each did cry, Musha, Paddy, good bye.
  What the devil made yez die, och hone!

Then with Paddy on their shoulders, off to the grave they
    flew,
And all the near beholders kick'd up such a philliloo,
Then they down'd Paddy with a whack,
And made the coffin crack,
And each one said, tell the truth, Paddy, are ye dead?
    What the devil made yez die, och hone!

———

LEAVE US A LOCK OF YOUR HAIR.

As sung by J. H. Ogden.—Air, Low-Backed Car.

"The stars are brightly shining, the birds are in the
    bowers,
The holy light of the moon shines bright on the beautiful
    sleeping flowers;
Then, Norah, are yez sleeping, or cannot you hear me
    speaking?
You know that my heart is breaking, for the love of you,
    Norah, dear!
Why can't you speak to me, darling mavrone?—are ye
    made of stick or stone?—
Or, like Venus of ould, so bright and so bould, are ye
    without a morsel of flesh or bone?

"There's not a star abroad, love, no sound comes on the ear,
Save that rogue of a breeze, that whispers the trees, till
    he makes them shake with fear;
And the flowers are gently creeping to the window where
    you're sleeping,
And they are not kept from peeping at your beauty, my
    Norah dear:
But it's yourself that's the hard-hearted soul, to keep me
    out here like an owl:
Sure, it's treatment too bad, for a true-hearted lad, to be
    served like that desolate fowl.

"You know the vow we made, love; you know we named
    the day;

Here I am now to keep the vow, and carry my love away.
Then, Norah, why be staying, for weeping or for praying?
There's danger in delaying: for, may be, I'd change my
mind;
And yez know, I'm a bit of a rake, and a trifle would
make me mistake;
And, but for your blue eye, I've a notion to try what sort
of an ould maid you'd make."

"Dermot, do not teaze me to be your bride to-night;
How could I bear my mother's tears, and my father's
scornful slight?
Then, Dermot, cease your wooing, or you'll really be my
ruin;
You'll be my life's undoing, if you're caught at the lattice-
gate!"
"Oh! for shame, with your foolish alarms; throw yourself into my arms·
Don't be waiting at all for your bonnet or shawl, they were
made but to cover your charms.

Just then a cloud arising across the moon was cast:
The casement opes, and anxious hopes make Dermot's
heart beat fast;
And then a form entrancing, half sinking, half advancing,
With her arm and bare neck glancing, she appears at the
lattice-gate;—
When a terrible arm in the air, seized the head of the
lover, quite bare,
And cried with a scoff, as Dermot ran off, "Would yez
leave us a lock of your hair?"

THE IRISH LOVE-LETTER.

Och! Judy, dear creature, she has won my sowl—
The thoughts of her eyes puts my heart in a fililoo;
By the side of my donkey I lay, cheek by jowl,
On a sheet of brown paper to write her a billy doo.

I had no pen, so made shift with a skewer,
  And thus I began all my mind to reveal :—
Och! Judy, says I, I've a mind to be sure,
  That you should become lovely Mistress O'Neal.
            Whack fal lal, fal, de ral, whack fal lal.

My father's a sempstress, makes clothes for the army,
  My mother's a coalman on Dublin quays;
And if you were with us, I know it would charm ye
  To see all our dacent and illegant ways.
Each day, for dinner, we've herrings or salmon—
  We eat our potatoes without any peel;
And so you may, Judy, without any gammon,
  If you will but become lovely Mistress O'Neal.
            Whack, &c.

Though my skewer's a bad pen you may judge of my
      knowledge,
  My penmanship, spelling, and books that I read;
I was brought up next door to great Trinity College,
  And learnt mathematical French and the creed.
If you can't read this letter the parson will do it,
  Och! Commong voo polty voo madamoyselle;
I can fight like the divil, and faith you shall know it!
  If you will but become lovely Mistress O'Neal.
            Whack, &c.

I love you, my jewel, although you are after
  That white headed Barney, the plasterer's son;
I'll show him my fist—that will show him his master,
  If you ever think of you two making one.
Och! if you but have him, by Jove he will catch it!
  I'll write him a challenge, though he be in jail;
And I'll break his nose so that he never will match it—
  Now won't you beccome lovely Mistress O'Neal?
            Whack, &c.

Then, if you won't have me, I'll lisht for a sodger,
  I'll be kilt and be prisoned,—och! then how will you
      feel?

sure whether you be a housekeeper or lodger,
    That you were not born to be Mistress O'Neal.
With my wounds and my wooden legs how I will haunt
    you.
    About twelve at midnight,—"Och murther!" you'll
        squeal,
When I tell you that ghosts and hobgoblins do want
    you,
    So no more at present, from Phelim O'Neal.
                                        Whack, &c.

BRYAN O'LYNN.

Bryan O'Lynn was a gentleman born,
He lived at a time when no clothes they were worn,
But as fashions walked out of course Bryan walked in,
Whoo! I'll soon lead the fashions, says Bryan O'Lynn.

Bryan O'Lynn had no breeches to wear,
He got a sheep skin for to make him a pair,
With the fleshy side out, and the woolly side in,
Whoo! they're pleasant and cool, says Bryan O'Lynn.

Bryan O'Lynn had no shirt to his back,
He went to a neighbor's and borrowed a sack,
Then he puckered the meal bag up under his chin,
Whoo! they'll take them for ruffles, says Bryan
    O'Lynn.

Bryan O'Lynn had no hat to his head,
He stuck on the pot being up to the dead,
Then he murdered a cod for the sake of its fin,
Whoo! 'twill pass for a feather, says Bryan O'Lynn.

Bryan O'Lynn was hard up for a coat,
He borrowed a skin of a neighboring goat,
With the horns sticking out from his oxters, and then,
Whoo! they'll take them for pistols, says Bryan
    O'Lynn.

Bryan O'Lynn had no stockings to wear,
He bought a rat's skin to make him a pair,
He then drew them over his manly shin,
Whoo! they're illegant wear, says Bryan O'Lynn.

Bryan O'Lynn had no brogue to his toes,
He hopped in two crab-shells to serve him for those,
Then he split up two oysters that matched like a
    twin,
Whoo! they'll shine out like buckles, says Bryan
    O'Lynn.

Bryan O'Lynn had no watch to put on,
He scooped out a turnip to make him a one,
Then he planted a cricket right under the skin,--
Whoo! they'll think it's a ticking, says Bryan
    O'Lynn.

Bryan O'Lynn to his house had no door,
He'd the sky for a roof, and the bog for a floor;
He'd a way to jump out, and a way to swim in,
Whoo! it's very convaynient, says Bryan O'Lynn.

Bryan O'Lynn, went a courting one night,
He set both the mother and daughter to fight:
To fight for his hand they both stripped to the skin,
Whoo! I'll marry you both, says Bryan O'Lynn.

Bryan O'Lynn his wife and wife's mother,
They all lay down in the bed together,
The sheets they were ould and the blankets were thin,
Lie close to the wall, says Bryan O'Lynn.

Bryan O'Lynn, his wife and wife's mother,
They all went home o'er the bridge together,
The bridge it broke down, and they all tumbled in,
Whoo! we'll go home by water, says Bryan 'OLynn.

BLACK TURF.

Air—"Buy a Broom."

Through Dublin, sweet city, I ramble my hearty,
With my kish of black turf for cold wintry noon,
They're cut from the bog of one Felix M'Carthy,
Arrah, now buy a cushla from your own Jack Muldoon.
Black turf, black turf, &c.

Spoken—Will you buy a mock? I will give you twenty-four black sods for one penny; devil the like of them ever was burnt before for heat, or boiling your pot; just take one of them in your hand, troth I am selling four pinnerth to Mistress Toole, of Coal Alley, and her decent husband, who is a knife grinder, declared to me that he can work without the dispensation of a candle, since he began to burn my black turf. Will you buy, Misther? do a-cushla. Will you, Mistress? do mam; don't be foolish to be spending your good looking money for coals; in troth, there wasn't luck nor grace in this country since the invention of coals, or any ill-lookin chimmistical commodity like them—will you buy a mock? Orra buy of Jack Muldoon his flaming black turf?

When your feet is all snow, and your toes are frost bitten,
Arrah then you'll discover my turf is your friend,
There's such light from the blaze that a letter I've written,
To my sweetheart Moll Grogan, for Christmas to spend.
Black turf, black turf, &c.

Spoken—Come now, girls, I am just come out, and the first that hansels me will get a fine sod over, orra jewels if you was after seeing the big boat-load I got consigned to myself, by my father-in-law, Marty Grogan. O millia murther! this is the lucky turf, the quality of Dublin shud be fond of; for the very bog it was cut from, moved half way to Dublin to see you, and only the *polis* overtook it, and wouldn't let it come any further that my father-in-law's it would be living in Dublin now, and all the young bogs would be Dublin people—this is the reason, I tell yez,

3

that all yez should lose no time to buy as much as you
can. Will you buy, Misther? I can only give twelve sods
for a penny of this turf, for you may depind on it, the
parents for them are well known ; the devil fire the sod of
this turf, but after its burnt, will walk out of the grate and.
get themselves blackened over and over again, fit for use,
and ready to boil any kittle, saucepan, or any of that family,
every bit as well as before, so that you see plainly you will
never have the same 'otunity any more of buying such
lucky turf. So yez won't buy—do you want any, my chap?
Is that a penny in your hand? Come and buy, now,
avic; O rista! crista! what bad times it is, they don't know
the vartue of the turf from the moving bog.

> Black turf, black turf, &c.

Orra gramachree avourneen, avourneen, avourneen,
Will you buy, avourneen, my moving black turf?
I am now nearly broke, to the bog I must hurry,
And to Jim Casey's berrin I'll be in time for to go,
Och, he died t other day, and many he's left sorry,
For he was a good hearted fellow (*cries*), but now he's laid
        low.

> Black turf, black turf, &c.

Spoken—Och! och! och! what sundry times those are
the world, in troth, is nothing but a boat-load of deceit,
and the honest people from the great gunchability of sick-
ness, are leaping up out of the world just like young trout
of a summer's day. Orra Jim Casey, avic, you've gone
without as much as bidding one of us good bye, (*cries*).
Och! heaven be your bed, Darby Quinn, if you war alive,
its yourself that would cry millia murther after poor Jim.
I would be on the vartue of my oath, if Moll Casey took
my advice, Jim would be at work to-day, the dirty sutrican,
I tould her to give him a little buttered punch, which
would be the means of conglomerating his bowels; but
stid of that, she gives him a skillet full of mouldy colcan-
non—Will you buy, &c.

BIDDY MAGEE.

Air.—" Rattlin', Rovin' Blade."

I was born in the town of Tip, so gay,
Where the boys they welt the flure away;
Faith, I fell in love, my boys, d'ye see,
An' the girl I lov'd was Biddy Magee.

I wint to the fair one summer's day,
Dress'd in my Sunday frieze so gay,
An' in a tint I wint so free;
And there I met with Biddy Magee.

I call'd for a naggin of the old ding dong,
Jist to give a polish to the song,
I paid for the same frank an' free;
And the first toothfull I gave was to Biddy Magee.

I gave her a chuck under the chin,
My blarney tale I did begin:
To be my wife she did agree,
So condescending was Biddy Magee.

Thin, my boys, a week after that,
Biddy she married her darlin' Pat;
The boys I invited to join in the spree,
Of the wedding of Pat an' Biddy Magee.

There was tall Maguire and Dinny O'Moore,
Phaly an' Tim to welt at the flure;
M'Gorman, the fiddler, who never could see;
He came to squint at Biddy Magee.

The whiskey wint round in quarts galore,
Those who were knocked up fell on the flure;
Thin Phaley an' Tim to kick up a spree,
Swore by dad, they'd have the first kiss from Biddy Magee

I bate the devils that very night,
And put the company all to flight;

Sis I, " My boys, you shall see
What a kiss you'll get from Biddy Magee."

We finished the row as it did begin,
Thin Biddy an' I put out the glim;
We wint to bed quite drunk, d'ye see—
An' there I 'gan huggin' Biddy Magee.

THE WIDDY McGINNESS'S RAFFLE.

Air—"The Ould Leather Breeches."

One Saturday night we'd a bit of a fight,
   I was dressed in my best, so genteelly;
While for company's sake in my fist did I take
   My ould-country blackthorn shillaly.
Going through Cherry street, there who should I meet
   But my countryman, Larry McGaflle?
"Arrah, Mickey!" says he, "will you take, do ye see,
   A ticket to go to a raffle?"
           Fal lal de ral lal, etc.

Says I, "Larry, begor, would ye tell me whot's for,
   Nor my mind with false fancies bewildher?"
"It's to bring out," says he, "from the ould counthry,
   Widdy McGinness and fourteen small childher.
The prize, you must know, is a fiddle and bow—
   'Twas presented by Mister Tim Whaffle;
The chairman is he of the grand com-mit-tee
   On the Widdy McGinness's raffle."

The quarter I spint, and with Larry I wint—
   From Oak street we turned to Cherry;
At each *shebeen* we'd stop for to take a small drop,
   By the time we got there we were merry.
As the dure we passed through, what a sight met my view!
   All my powers of description 'twould baffle:
In all sorts of dress, full three hundred—or less,
   Were at Widdy McGinness's raffle!

There was Teddy McVay, and Barney McShay,
   Larry Brogan and Mickey McConnell;

There was Long Jerry Ryan and Pether O'Brian,
   Mike Faygan and Patsey O'Donnell;
There was big Biddy Burke and Miss Judy McGurk,
   Widdy Casey and Kitty McGraffil;
There was Molly Mulvany, Miss Flynn and her granny,
   At Widdy McGinness's raffle.

There was Murty McGool, there was Paddy O'Toole,
   Conny Regan and Malachi Keller;
Moll Lynch and her brothers, wid twenty score others,
   In Michael McLaughlin's cellar.
Whin the dice were brought on, then the rattling begun,
   Till Barney McShay took a shuffle:
"Two sixes, a five! be the powers alive,
   I've all soorts of good luck at the raffle!"

Says Teddy, "That's mine! faix, I bate you that time."
   Says Barney, "You lie like the divil!"
But Judy in haste then jumped up to make pace,
   Saying, "Och! Barney, dear, don't be oncivil."
But Teddy stepped out and hit him a clout,
   Saying, "My luck you've been trying to baffle."
From Barney he quick got a belt of a stick,
   And the ructions comminced at the raffle.

Soon each faction enraged were in battle engaged,
   And the blood it began to flow freely:
But the whole of the crew couldn't lather *us two*—
   That's meself and my blackthorn shillaly.
My stick got excited, it wanted to fight,
   It longed to take part in the battle;
It hit Shaughnessy's Ted such a belt on the head,
   That it knocked him stone blind at the raffle.

But soon the polace for keeping the pace,
   To the sate of war marched in a body:
Every poor divil they caught, to the station they brought,
   Blind drunk and brim full of the toddy.
To the justice we wint, and for tin days he sint
   Up to prison meself and McGaffle;
  3*

But a vow now I'll give, that aslong as I live —
  I'll be damned if I go to a raffle!
            Fal lal de ral lal, etc.

CORPORAL CASEY.

When I was at home I was merry and frisky,
My dad kept a pig, and my mother sold whiskey,
My uncle was rich, but could never be aisy,
Till I was enlisted by Corporal Casey.

Spoken.—The Corporal was an odd sort of a man, and
he came every morning into my mother's house, and take
his drops of calamity water, as he used to call it; and then
he drew up a long big form before the fire, and he'd sit
himself down, and take me upon his knee, and tell me of
all the Spanish generals he killed, and all the French battles that he'd won. Now, you must know, that I felt a
sort of sneaking kindness to a red coat; so says I to the
corporal one morning, would you have any objection to
make me a bit of a soldier? Musha avourneen, says the
corporal, I don't care if I do. So with that he tips me a
bright shilling and away I goes to his

Rub a dub, row de dow, Corporal Casey,
Oh, rub a dub, row de dow, Corporal Casey,
My dear little Sheelah, I thought would turn crazy,
Oh, when I trudged away with tough Corporal Casey,
I marched from Kilkenny, and as I was thinking,
On Sheelah, my heart in my bosom was sinking;
But soon I was forced to look fresh as a daisy,
For fear of a drubbing from Corporal Casey.

Spoken.—Well, there we were, all drawn out upon the
parade, rank and file, as they call it—so says I to myself,
Patrick, my honey, the best thing you can do is, to make
friends of the corporal. Now, I knew if anything could get
over him at all at all, 'twould be the thoughts of the *ouneen.*
So over I goes to him—Morrow to you, Mr. Corporal, says

I, speaking very dignified to him, would your honor's reverence and glory like to take a drop of anything to drink this morning? By the powers, says he. I don't care if I do. So over I goes to the sign of the Sack and Water—just such another little hole in the wall as my poor ould mother kept in her time—God rest her soul she's dead and gone—well, there I calls for three naggins of whiskey, and the devil burn me if I ever get one drop of it. Well, over we comes again upon the parade, rank and file, as they call it—so, right about left, says the corporal. Now you must know that my left arm was hanging over my right shoulder that morning. So over the Corporal comes to me, and he gives me such a *loudogue* under the ear, that och, by the powers, it made me caper to his

Rub a dub, row de dow, Corporal Casey,
Och, rub a dub, row de dow, Corporal Casey,
The devil go with him, I ne'er could be *aisey*,
He stuck in my skirts so, ould Corporal Casey.

We went into battle, I took the blows fairly,
That fell on my pate, but they bothered me rarely;
And who should the first be that dropt, who ain't plase ye,
It was my good friend honest Corporal Casey.

Spoken.—When the corporal fell, he was down—there he lay *superficially* on the broad of his back, like a half-crown; hurrah, corporal! says I, are you dead?—spaking low and aisy for fear of waking the poor cratur, are ye dead? says I, are ye dead, an' be damned, says I—will ye speak? Then I thought he was dead, sure enough—then I listened a bit awhile, and I thought I heard the corporal snore. Are ye dead? says I, again. Ah, no, says he, I'm not dead, but I'm kilt and speechless; but if you had any regard for me in my lifetime, be after looking for my head, and place it between my shoulders; as it is my only wish that I should be buried in a Christian-like sort of a manner. Then says I, as it is your only request, it shall be done. So away I trots all over the field in search of his napper, but the devil a head could I find of the corporal's at all at

all. So I was just returning with the good news to inform
him that I couldn't find it—when where the devil do you
think I saw it? why between the tall legs of a grenadier
who had just fell before him. Now you must know I had
a pretty decent knowledge of the corporal's head, for in his
days he wore a large red-raw pimple on the top of his nose;
here Mr. Corporal, says I, here's your head. Ramnation
seize your soul, don't ye know your own nose? Ramnation
seize your soul, says he, 'tis no head of mine. Head or no
head, says I, no other head you'll get from me; so I threw
his head in his face, and away run from his

Rub a dub, row de dow, Corporal Casey,
Och, rub a dub, row de dow, Corporal Casey,
And now my dear friends, I come here for to *plase* ye!
After eight years campaigning with Corporal Casey

THE HARD-HEARTED MOLLY CAREW

Written by S. Lover, Esq.

Och hone!
Oh, what will I do?
Sure my love is all crost,
Like a bud in the frost,
And there's no use at all
In my going to bed;
For 'tis dhrames, and not slape
That comes into my head!
And 'tis all about you,
My sweet Molly Carew,
And indeed 'tis a sin and a shame
You're complatur than nature
In every feature,
The snow can't compare
To your forehead so fair,
And I rather would spy
Just one blink of your eye,

Than the purtiest star,
That shines out of the sky,
Though by this and by that,
For the matter o' that,
You're more distant by far than that same.
  Och hone! wirasthrew!
      I am alone
In this world without you!

      Och hone!
But why should I speak
Of your forehead and eyes,
When your nose it defies
Paddy Blake, the schoolmaster,
    To put it in rhyme?
Though there's one Burke, he says
    Would call it a *snub*-lime.
And then for your cheek,
Troth, would take him a week
Its beauties to tell,
    As he'd rather;
Then your lips, oh, machree!
    In their beautiful glow,
They a pattern might be,
For the cherries to grow!
'Twas an apple that tempted
    Our mother, we know—
For apples were scarce,
    I suppose, long ago,
But at this time of day,
'Pon my conscience I'll say,
Such cherries might tempt
    A man's father.
    Och hone! wirasthrew
      I'm alone
In the world without you

      Och hone!
By the man in the moon!
You teaze me all ways,
That a woman can plaze;

For you dance twice as high,
With that thief, Pat Magee,
As when you take share
    Of a jig, dear, with me
Though the piper I hate;
For fear the old chate
    Wouldn't play your favorite tune
And when you're at mass,
My devotion you crass,
For 'tis thinking of you
I am, Molly Carew;
While you wear on purpose
    A bonnet so deep,
That I can't at your swate
Pretty face get a peep.
Oh, lave off that bonnet.
    Or else I'll lave on it,
The loss of my wandering sowl
    Och hone! like an owl!
        Day is night,
Dear, to me without you!

        Och hone!
Don't provoke me to do it,
For there's girls by the score,
That love me, and more—
And you'd look very queer,
    If some morning you'd meet
My wedding all marching
    In pride down the street,
Troth! you'd open your eyes,
And you'd die of surprise,
To think 'twasn't you
    Was to come to it,
And faith! Katty Neale,
And her cow, I'll go bail,
Would jump, if I'd say,
"Katty Neale, name the day,"
And though you're fair and fresh
As the blossoms in May

And she's short and dark,
   Like a cowld winter's day;
Yet if you don't repent
Before Easter—when Lent
Is over, I'll marry
For spite.
   Och hone! and when I die for you,
'Tis my ghost that you'll see every night.

THE COBLER.

I'm a roving sporting blade,
   Likewise a jolly young fellow,
My spirits they are sunk,
   And I wish to keep them mellow.
               Rantana, &c.

I went to her father's house,
   Of him I asked a favor ;
He gave me his consent,
   And told me I should have her.
               Rantana, &c.

He gave me fifty guineas in gold,
   Likewise a stock of leather,
And a lot of old shoes,
   And I stuck them all together.
               Rantana, &c.

Come Sal, wax me up this thread,
   You are my dearest Sally,
Pay will come due next week,
   And we'll blot the huckster's tally.
               Rantana, &c.

If my wife should prove with child,
   Surely it would be my ruin,
For then I must lay down,
   My own two hands a sewing.
               Rantana, &c.

But stop, I've lost my wax,
  And I don't know what's become of it,
And worse than all I've got the tax,
  Oh, I believe this is some of it.

Rantana, &c.

Bad fortune to staggering Bob,
  The plague light on him for ever,
I'd rather have a large sheep's nob,
  With a good sound heart and liver.

Rantana, &c.

DENNIS M'CASTER, THE IRISH SCHOOLMASTER.

Then Dennis M'Caster the Irish schoolmaster,
  No one could teach faster the English tongue;
He was poet and punster, and by every youngster,
  O'er the province of Munster his praises were sung.
Rare scholars had Denny, from Cork and Kilkenny,
  From Kilbrain sure many did flock to his school,
Where he o'er the sly ones, the Neills and O'Brians,
  And wild Irish lions, triumphant did rule.

Spoken—Doctor Dennis M'Caster neither taught on Bell's nor the Lancasterian system. Faith, they were both one to him, but on a plan of his own, which he called the Munsterman's, or the true Irish system. Master Felix O'Brian, said he, before you do go *down*, come *up* and say your lesson, for you are my best scholar. Now, what's the first figure of your A B C? I don't know, sir. You don't know. For shame, Felix; what does my donkey often get to eat? Nothing, sir. Nothing, and what else? Water, sir. Arrah, does he get nothing but *water* to eat. Yes, sir, pitatee *pails*. Pitatee-pails, and what else? Hay. That's a good boy; go on. I can't sir. You can't! remember you're my head scholar, and tell me what bird is it that lays the honey? Bee. B, that's right; then *be* a good boy, my honey, and go on. I can't, sir. You can't! a pretty tale will be made of my head scholar, and I can make neither head nor tail of him. Can't you tell me where all the salt fish comes from? Yes, sir, from Judy Donovan, the fishmonger, sir. And where else? From the salt sea, sir. Arrah! can't you say C without the salt, as it should be. Yes, sir, sea without salt, as it should be. Go on, you bogtrotter. I can't sir. You can't, tell me, my jewel, how often do I flog you? Every day, sir. Can't you say *day* alone. Yes, sir. Go on. I can't, sir. Arrah, what sex am I of? Faith, sir, I don't know; you know better than I, why do you ask? Because I want to know. *She* sex, sir? No. *He*, sir. E, that's right, my boy. What's next? I can't tell—yes, sir, I can, F. Bravo! go on. I can't, sir. What does carman Pat say to his horse? Gee, Thunder, now. Can't you say G without thunder, now? Yes, sir; Gee an' no thunder now. Go on. I can't, sir. Now, tell me how many of you learn at my academy? Aich one of us. Can't you say H, and not one of us. Yes, sir, aich and not one of us. An' by the holy poker, I'll make aich of you remember it, like the great actor on the stage used to say to the Munster man. I'll fill your bones full of H's (aches), and by the powers, that will be or way to make you a man of letters.

Then success to M'Caster, the Irish schoolmaster,
    For sure such a pastor the world never saw;
And long life to the dry land of th' Emerald island—
    Faith, but I love you! och, Erin-go-bragh.
Though Dan was a gen'us, I must say between us
    He was not a Venus in shape or in air;
For Mrs. Nature, when she made me the teacher,
    Did not for each feature take at all any care;
His eye was a skew one, his nose was a blue one,
    His mouth was a true one from ear to ear.;
Yet vanity drove him—like many above him,
    If folks did not love him, he would make them fear.

Spoken.—Come and go on with your lesson. What's next to H? I don't know. You don't know. Can't you tell me what your old aunt's got by the side of her nose? A

4

carbuncle, sir. And what else? A long bristle, sir. What
else? Oh, it's an eye, sir. Aye that's right; go on. I
can't, sir? Can't you tell me how your mother opens the
door? Puts her finger in the hole, sir. Arrah! what does
she lock it with? A kay with a lucky stone tied to it.
Can't you say K without lucky stone? Kay, and no lucky
stone. Go on. I can't, sir. What measure is that next
the yard? Yard, sir, the pig-stye, sir. Arrah, what letter's
that a yard and a quarter long? An' ell, sir. L, an by the
hoakey! such a decent sized one required a whole sheet
to write it upon. Go on: what's next to L? Hell, a school,
sir. Nonsense, what letter? I don't know, sir. Can't
you tell me what your mother does with your shirts?
Shirts, I've got none, sir. What does she do with your
father's then? Pawn them, sir. For shame, Felix,
don't expose your relations; she only lends them to
your uncle. What does she do when she makes them?
Hem, sir. M, that's true; go on. I can't. Which of my
fowls lays the large duck eggs? The-cock-a-doodle-doo,
sir. But who's cock-a-doodle's wife? Hen, sir. N, good;
go on, what's next? I can't say that, sir. You can't! I'll
bring it out of you, my boy; take that thump. (Oh!) O,
I thought I could bring it out; now wipe your nose, and
tell me what's the next one? P. Q, sir. That's right, my
boy; always mind your P's and Q's, and then you may go
aud sit down to sing

Success to M'Caster, &c.

Our hero, M'Caster, the wise Irish pastor,
    A shocking disaster did meet in his youth,
For, fighting a duel with Paddy O'Trowel,
    A shillelah so cruel knocked out every tooth.
Their shillelahs were oaken a word was not spoken,
    Till one leg was broken by Paddy to two;
Pat then beat no further, for Dan hallooed murther!
    And swore he was kilt from his hat to his shoe.

Spoken.—Master Felix O'Brian, come and begin the end
of your lesson. Where did I leave you? At the P's and
Q's, sir. Well, now come back and go forward: that's the
way to get on, my boy. What's next to Q? P, sir. What

else? I don't know, sir. What did the justice put your
father in? The stocks, sir. And what else! The army,
sir. And what's the first letter of army? Ar, sir. Good;
go on. I can't, sir. What is that like a pot-hook and
hanger? That's your left-hand leg, sir. Left-hand leg,
arrah! then what is my left-hand leg like? A crooked S,
sir. Go on. I can't sir. What does your mother drink
out of the tea-pot on a morning? Whiskey. What else
at breakfast? Tea dust, sir. Arrah! can't you say tea,
without dust, as it should be. Go on, you devil of a dust-
man, and tell me what's next? I can't sir. You can't—
who struck you just now? Your mutton fist, sir. Mutton
fist! and who does my mutton fist belong to? You, sir.
U, go on. I can't sir. What did the pig say to the
Frenchman? We, sir. Och! faith, 'twas a learned pig.
Go on. I can't, sir. What does your uncle knock the
trees down with? With an axe, sir. X, go on. What's
next? I can't say that, sir. Why can't you say it? I
can't say why, sir. Go on; perhaps you'll remember the
last letter first. Yes, sir, Y, sir. Ho! you've remembered
the first at last; now what's next? I don't know, sir.
You don't. Can you tell me what part of Paddy's body I
knocked a hole in? His head, sir. Z, that's right, my
boy, you'll make a clever man. Now go home, and write
upon your paper skull, a wise head (Y Z), whilst you sing.

Success to M'Caster, &c.

FROM MUNSTER I CAME.

Air.—"Patrick's Day in the Morning."

From Munster I came, and I went into Leinster,
I met with a dame, and they called her a spinster,
I sat down on a stool in the corner fornenced her,
On Patrick's day in the morning.
Says I, my dear jewel, I'm the boy that has plenty
Of praties and cabbage, and all other dainties.
I'm comely and clane, and just turned one and twenty;

I've bullocks and cows, and things worth your attention,
I've great things, and small things, and things I won't
  mention,
Arrah, my darlint, I'll treat you with all condescension,
  On Patrick's day in the morning.

Ah, aheagar, says she, though I'm not in a hurry,
If along with yourself a short time I would tarry,
Then what d'ye think if myself you would marry,
  On Patrick's day in the morning?
For I've two hundred guineas, a two-year old heifer,
A pig and a goat, that's both comely and clever;
On a Sunday I ride with my new coat and beaver—
  Arrah, boy, will you have me, but will you remember
  To use me genteel, for you know I'm but tender?
  She was threescore and ten long after November,
  On Patrick's day in the morning.

Now she had but one tooth. and that same was quite rotten,
We struck up the match, and to church we went trotting.
Sure we vowed and we swore things that shant be forgot-
  ten,
  On Patrick's day in the morning,
But just coming home, as you know it's our nature,
We went into a shebeen house to get a drop of the crea-
  ture,
My wife then she swigged it, bad luck to the neater;
  But you see on the road home we met with a river,
  I forgot my politeness, and jumped it quite clever.
  My wife tumbled in, and I lost her forever,
  On Patrick's day in the morning.

———

I COME FROM THE LAND OF THE PATS AND PITATEES.

I come from the land of the pats and pitatees,
                          Tidhery idhery tow row row,
Where we're fond of good things, and of coorse, love the
  ladies,   Tid, &c.

But I was unlike every boy of my nation,
Resisting forever love's fatal temptation,
In the noise of the dhrum drowning love's botheration.

> Tid, &c.

Till one day I discovered a lady like Venus,

> Tid, &c.

Her eyes like the stars in King Charles' wain is

> Tid, &c.

On the head of my dhrum down she sat on a large hill,
And I courted her there till she vowed she was partial,
Can I ever forget that sweet dhrum-head court-martial.

> Tid, &c.

Then come with your soger, my own little charmer,

> Tid, &c.

To keep us from sorrow, good humor's the armor,

> Tid, &c.

Tho' poor, I am merry, i never look ginn,—
We shall never want bread if with me you will come—
When your hungry I'll give you fresh rolls on my drum

I CAME FROM THE ROAR.

Air.—"Kitty's Rambles from Youghal."

I came from the Roar, in the county Kilkenny,
Not a rag on my back; in my purse not a penny;
At handling the boulthaun I was counted with any
  That ever came down from the Colliery Hills.
The girls all pressed me, hugged, and caressed me,
Peelers would chase me, proctors would trace me,
I drank; but that's all that could ever disgrace me;
  And still I'm pursued with all kinds of ills.

I went to the Guards, and ax'd them to bind me
Awhile to the Queen, as poor Jude was behind me;
They swore that they would, if in sound wind they'd
    me,
  So off to the doctors they trudged my own self.
  4*

" Come, peel off your duds, sir! here, corporal, the suds,
     sir!
Wash him down from the crown; he's wild from the
     woods, sir.
Then give him a dose for to scour his blood, sir:
     And take him to drill—the unfortunate elf."

They hoist me away, ogh murder! to swear me,
They gave me the book, shure I swore d——l tare me,
If ever I thought 'twas so hard to prepare me,
     To handle the gun in defence of the queen.
" Her majesty's heirs then," said sarjeants in pairs then,
" You'll swear to maintain, over field, flood and main,
          then—'
" Ogh, for sartain," said I, " and 'twill give me no pain,
     then,
     If you maintain Judy at home on the plain."

They dressed myself out as clean as a whistle,
My livery the shamrock, the rose, and the thistle;
My prayer book was neither the Path, Key or Missal;
     But the gun I must live with in place of my wife.
They drilled me, half killed me, they learned me to march
          so;
They stocked me, they knocked—I swore that was no go—
I up with my fist, then a regular brain blow,
     Brought down the sarjeant most short of his life.

They hoist me away to the guard house next minute,
And never cried crack till they lodged me safe in it,
Ogh! the mischief take grief on the wings of the linnet,
     If ever I learn such tricks any more.
So a fig for your laws, your starved Johnny Raws,
I'm shot, but you gave my *lashing*, and cause
No longer to earn such bloody applause—
     So hurra for my own native cot on the Roar.

IRISH ENGLISH SCOTCHMAN.

AIR—Push about the Jorum.

My father was an Irishman,
  And born in sweet Kilkenny,
My mother was in England born,
  In Lincolnshire so funny;
In Scotland they were put to bed,
  Nine months ere they saw me, sir,
And as for Ireland home they sailed,
Myself was born at sea, sir.

CHORUS:

My country so, I cannot know,
  So comical my lot's man,
I'll prove myself where'er I go,
  An English Irish Scotchman.

English independence with
  My mother's milk imbibed, sir,
And gen'rous Irish principle,
  My father's rules prescribed, sir;
Ere I was born, I got a stock
  Of honest Scottish pride, too—
My heart's as free as my native sea,
  For friendship just as wide too.
        My country though, &c.

A soldier marshalled in the ranks,
  'Twas on a grand review day,
Our captain stepped up to me—
  "What countryman are you, pray?"
"What countryman—why would you know,
  D'ye think it values much, man?
With you I'll go to fight the foe,
  Or Spaniard, French, or Dutchman."
        My country though, &c

From war returned, and having saved
  A competence for life, sir,

To share it and enjoy it too,
   I needs must take a wife, sir.
" Your parish, friend, I first must know "
   The cautious parson cried, sir:
" As I for all fought 'gainst the foe,
   My parish pays no tithe, sir."
               My country though, &c

May Irish, English, Scottish hearts,
   Be linked to one another;
The shamrock, rose, and thistle, too,
   Be blended altogether.
May Victoria's kingdom never fall,
   Supported long by such men;
And may her subjects, one and all,
   Be Irish English Scotchmen.
               My country though, &c.

PADDY HEGARTY'S LEATHER BREECHES.

It was at the sign of the Bell, on the road to Clonmel,
   Paddy Hegarty kept a neat shebeen;
He sold pig's meat and bread, kept a good lodgin' bed,
   And so well liked round the country had been;
Himself and his wife both struggled thro' life,
   In the week days Pat mended the ditches,
But on Sunday he dressed in a coat of the best,
   But his pride was his old leather breeches.
             Fol de rol, &c

For twenty-one years at least, so it appears,
   His father those breeches had run in—
The morning he died he to his bedside
   Called Paddy, his beautiful son, in!
Advice then he gave ere he went to the grave—
   He bid him take care of his riches—
Says he it's no use to pop into my shoes,
   But I wish you'd step into my breeches.

Last winter, the snow, left provisions so low,
  Poor Paddy was eat out complately;
The snow coming down he could not go to town,
  Thoughts of hunger soon bothered him greatly.
One night as he lay dreaming away,
  About creedougs, frogs and witches,
He heard an uproar just outside of the door,
  And he jumpt to streel on his ould breeches.

Says Bryan M'Quirk, with a voice like a Turk,
  Paddy come get us some eating,
Says big Andy Moore, I'll burst open the door,
  For this is no night to be waiting;
Scarce had he spoke when the door went in broke,
  And they crowded round Paddy like leeches,
By their great mortal gob, if he didn't get them prog,
  They'd eat him clean out of his breeches.

Now Paddy in dread slipt into his bed,
  That held Judy, his darling wife in,
And there he agreed to get them a feed—
  He slipt out and brought a big knife in;
He took up the waist of his breeches—the beast,
  And cut out the buttons and stitches,
He cut them in stripes by the way they were tripes,
  And boiled them, his ould leather breeches.

When the tripes were stew'd on a dish they were strew'd,
  The boys all cried out, Lord be thanked,
But Hagerty's wife was afraid of her life,
  She thought it high time for to shank it.
To see how they smiled, for they thought Pat had boiled
  Some mutton and beef of the richest,
But little they knew it was leather burgoo.
  That was made out of Paddy's ould breeches.

They wollip'd the stuff, says Andy, it's tough,
  Says Paddy you're no judge of mutton;
When Bryan M'Quirk, on the point of a fork,
  Lifted up a big ivory button!

Says Darby, what's that? sure I thought it was fat,
  Bryan leaps on his legs, and he screeches,
By the powers above, I was trying to shove
  My teeth through the flap of his breeches!

They made at Pat, he was gone out of that,
  He run when he found them all rising—
Says Bryan, make haste, and go for the priest,
  By the holy saint Jackstones I'm poisoned!
Revenge for the joke they had, for they broke
  All the chairs, tables, bowls and dishes;
And from that very night they will knock out your day-
    light,
  If they catch you with a pair of leather breeches.

JOHNNY M'CLUSKY.

Air—"Savourneen Dheelish."

The moments were happy when we got married,
Johnny M'Clusky and Sweet Molly Crow,
'Twas in a neat sedan to church I saw my Molly carried,
                              Johnny, &c.
What a happy moment when first I saw your face, love,
When I stooped down in the puddle to hand you up your
    lace glove,
I stepped up so genteelly, and bowed with such a grace,
    dove,
                              Johnny, &c.
What a handsome leg you had the night you danced at the
    ball,
                              Johnny, &c.
'Twas then I felt love's fatal darts, as you danced down
    with Johnny Hall.
                              Johnny, &c.
When you were tired dancing, 'twas on my arm you re-
    clined,
When I opened the window, to let in the gentle wind,

You looked at me so lovingly, and spoke so sweet and so
    refined.

Johnny, &c.

When first we set up house-keeping, 'twas in Dirty-lane,
    dear;

Johnny, &c.

We sold butter, turf, freestone, and pins, and kept a cellar
    clean, dear,

Johnny, &c.

And with our little profit it's we that lived contented,
Till a storm blew down the house that we so lately rented,
Besides seven and twenty pounds, but hang it mam you
    spend it.

Johnny, &c.

KATTY MOONEY.

I courted Katty Mooney dear,
    A girl so nate and cosie,
Her eyes they were both bright and clear,
    And her cheeks were red and rosy.
I bought a pig to live with us,
    I got a stick to mind it ;
'Twas a clever pig, but like the rest,
    It carried its tail behind it,
Oh, hubbuboo, &c.

When we were wed, and soon made one
    In love we made a dozen,
Until she brought to town with her
    Her thirty-second cousin ;
I made him eat, I made him drink,
    With compliments he lined me,
But the reason why I never could find,
    Till one day he stayed behind me.
Oh, hubbuboo, &c

I don't know what, when I came back,
    I wish I had not seen them.

For there they were giving smack for smack
  And the pig was sitting between them;
He ran away, och och hubbuboo!
  May the devil catch and bind him,
And my wife may go to the devil too,
  If they'd left the pig behind them.
Oh, hubbuboo, &c.

MOLLY MALONE.

By the big hill of Howth,
  That's a bit of an oath,
That to swear by it I'm loth,
  To the heart of a stone,
But be poison my drink,
  If I sleep, snore, or wink,
Once forgetting to think,
  Of your lying alone,
Sweet Molly, Sweet Molly Malone,
Sweet Molly, sweet Molly Malone.
Och! its how, &c.

Och! it's now I'm in love,
  Like a beautiful dove,
That sits cooing above,
  In the boughs of a tree!
It's myself I'll soon smother,
  In something or other,
Unless I can bother
  Your heart to love me,
Sweet Molly, sweet Molly Malone,
Sweet Molly, sweet Molly Malone.
Och! its how, &c.

I can see if you smile,
  Though I'm off half a mile,
For my eyes all the while,
  Keep along with my head;
And my head you must know,

When from Molly I go,
Takes his leave with a bow,
And remains in my stead.
          Och! its how, &c.

Like a bird I could sing,
  In the month of the spring,
But it's no such a thing,
  I'm quite bothered and dead.
Och! I'll roar and I'll groan,
  My sweet Molly Malone,
'Till I'm bone of your bone,
  And asleep in your bed.
          Och! its how, &c.

MEET ME, MISS MOLLY MALONE.

Meet me, Miss Molly Malone,
  At the grove at the end of the vale;
But be sure that you don't come alone,
  Bring a pot of your master's strong ale;
With a nice bit of beef and some bread,
  Some pickled or cucumbers green,
Or a nice little dainty pig's head,
  'Tis the loveliest tit-bit e'er seen,
Then meet me Miss Molly Malone.

Pastry may do for the gay,
  Old maids may find comfort in tea;
But there's something about ham and beef,
  That agrees a deal better with me.
Remember my cupboard is bare,
  Then come, if my dear life you prize,
I'd have lived the last fortnight on air,
  But you sent me two nice mutton pies,
Then meet me, Miss Molly Malone.

5

PAT AND HIS LEATHER BREECHES.

Although a simple clown,
  My life pass'd sweet as honey,
'Till daddy died in town,
  And left me all his money;
Some twenty pounds or more,
  With harrows, ploughs and ditches,
With grunters half a score,
  And a pair of leather breeches.
            Rumpty, bumpty, &c.

As pleased I was as fun,
  And dressed myself up natty;
Thinks I, the girls each one,
  Must think I very pretty;
With fortune quite content,
  Grief gave my heart no twitches;
To church on Sunday went,
  To sport my leather breeches!
            Rumpty, bumpty, &c.

But coming home, oh! dear,
  Some lads did jeer and flout me,
They filled my mind with fear,
  As they all flocked about me;
They 'gainst me did conspire,
  Soused me in ponds and ditches,
And soon with mud and mire,
  They daubed my leather breeches.
            Rumpty, bumpty, &c

I next did go to woo
  A damsel young and dapper;
But she at I looked blue,
  And ding dong went her clapper.
Says she, " I hate your plan,
  My heart agin your riches,
'Cause I can't bear a man,
  As wears them leather breeches."
            Rumpty, bumpty, &c.

To Dublin I went off,
   My spirits just to rally,
But each one did me scoff,
   In street, and lane, and alley.
My woes came on by halves,
   I got insulting speeches,
One fellow bawled out " calves!"
   Another "twig his breeches!"
             Rumpty, bumpty, &c.

A lass I met one night,
   As I for fun was dodging,
I thought myself all right,
   And with her took my lodging.
Next morn how I did curse,
   The girls and all such witches,
When I found she'd boned my purse,
   My watch, and leather breeches.
             Rumpty, bumpty, &c.

I left the house quite hurt,
   It rained and blew together ;
Exposed all in my shirt,
   I were to wind and weather.
The woman from me fled,
   I did not rue my riches,
But I'd have given my head,
   To have my leather breeches.
             Rumpty, bumpty, &c.

A poliss man past by,
   On duty never dozing,
And off to quod hiked I,
   My person for exposing !
The justice spoke his will,
   And with upbraiding speeches,
He sent me to the mill,
   All through my leather breeches.
             Rumpty, bumpty, &c.

But now once more I'm free,
   And by the coach to-morrow,

I will from Dublin flee,
    And try to drown my sorrow,
Once more to plough I'll go,
    A fig for pride or riches,
No more I'll be a beau,
    Or sport a leather breeches.
            Rumpty, bumpty, &c

THE FLAMING O'FLANAGANS.

Written by R. N. Shannon, Esq.

Oh, now I'm of age, and come into my property,
    Divil a hap'orth I'll think of but fun,
'Tis myself 'll be putting the ladies in *joppardy*,
    Just for to prove I'm my daddy's own son.
Ochone! Miss Malone, I'll tayche you some civility;
    Judy O'Doody escape—if you can,
I'm the boy that'll show yez the sweet sensibility,
    Lovin' most women, and fearing no man,
For that was the way with all the O'Flanagans,
    From the first bud of them down to myself,
And wasn't my mother besides of the Branagans,
    Why shouldn't I be a comical elf?
Oh, the racing and koorsing (*coursing*),
    And hunting and shooting,
The clattering of glasses, and batt'ring of skulls,
    The dances, where I'll be upon the best footing
With Irish Miss Murphies, and English Miss Bulls;
    The nate little parties of pleasure we'll rowl to,
The rows and the *ructions*, and divil knows what,
    The Dunns that I'll bate black and blue, by my soul too,
And the jules (*duels*) that I'll ind (*end*) wud (*with*) the very
        first shot,
    Hurroo! that was the way with the Flaming O'Flana-
        gans,
From the first illigant boys of the name,
    And wasn't my mother besides of the Branagans,
Why shouldn't I be a cock of the game?

ENCORE VERSES.

(*To a side box.*)

Do yez hear how I'm bothered by all these quare vaga-
bones,
  Shouting encore twice as loud as they can?

(*To the upper gallery.*)

Paddy Flinn, I'll be bound I'll give you a sore bag o' bones,
  If you come down and turn out like a man.
Do yez think I can stay here till morning divarting yez,
  While my nate jug of punch is cooling inside?
Good night, boys, you know that I'm sorry for parting yez,
  But the *loves of the spirits* was always my pride!
Hurroo! for that was the way *wud* the Flaming O'Flana-
gans,
  From the first terrible boy of the name,
They bet (*beat*) all the Hannigans, Langans, and Lannigans,
  Drinking and fighting like cocks of the game.

DUBLIN LASSES.

Air.—"Roy's Wife."

Cupid to fulfil a duty,
  Lately from Idalia passes;
Hovering o'er the isle of beauty,
  Gave the palm to Dublin lasses.
    O, the dear delighting lasses,
    Who compare with Dublin lasses,
    Wit and beauty both combine,
    And sweetly shine in Dublin lasses.

Venus with a view to teaze him,
  Sent him next to Mount Parnassus,
De'il a damsel there could please him,
  Like our charming Dublin lasses.
        O, the dear, delighting. &c.

Love is theirs, best boon of nature,
  Tendered by the kindred graces,

5*

Each endearing glance and feature
  Binds the heart to Dublin lasses.
            O, the dear, delighting, &c.

Music may have charms for many,
  Others stifle care o'er glasses,
My delight and boast is Fanny,
  Fairest of the Dublin lasses,
            O, the dear, delighting, &c.

Sigh who will for golden treasure,
  Mine's a gem that gold surpasses,
Fanny's smiles give wealth and pleasure,
  Gifts reserved for the Dublin lasses.
            O, the dear, delighting, &c.

THE BOYS OF THE IRISH BRIGADE.

What for should I sing you of Roman or Greek,
  Or the boys we hear tell of in story,
Come match me for fighting, for frolic or freak,
  An Irishman's reign in his glory.
For Ajax and Hector and bold Agamemnon,
  Were up to the tricks of our trade, O?
But the rollicking boys for war, women and noise,
  Are the boys of the Irish brigade, O.

What for should I sing you of Helen and Troy,
  Or the mischief that came by her flirting;
There's Biddy M'Clinch, the pride of Fermoy,
  Twice as much of a Helen that's certain.
Then for Venus Medicis, or Queen Cleopatra,
  Bad luck to the word could be said, O,
By the rollicking boys for war, women and noise,
  The boys of the Irish brigade, O.

What for should I sing you of classical fun,
  Or of games whether Grecian or Persian;

Sure the Curragh's the place where the knowing one's
    done,
  And Mallow that flogs for divarsion ;
For fighting, for drinking, for women and all,
  No times like our times e'er were made, O,
By the rollicking boys, for war, women and noise,
  The boys of the Irish Brigade, O.

THE YOUNG IRISH GENTLEMAN.

AIR.—"The Fine Old English Gentleman."

I'll sing you a modern song, wrote by a modern pate,
Of a gay young Irish nobleman, who holds a fine estate ;
And who cuts away through thick and thin, at a very
    slashing rate—
For a wager in his drawing-room, leaped o'er a five-barr'd
    gate,
Like a gay young Irish gentleman, all of the present time.

His walls so old, are hung around with boxing-gloves and
    sticks,
Wrenched knockers—police batons—the produce of his
    night's tricks :
And there his lordship puffs cigars with a heart both light
    and free ;—
As church bells toll the midnight hour he strolls forth
    for a spree,
Like a gay young Irish gentleman, all of the present time.

If any new policeman dared to stand but in his way,
He'd knock him down—"Damn me, come on, I only ask
    fair play."
Off goes his coat, down goes his man, who deplores a
    broken nose,
Our hero laughs, throws down ten pounds, to compensate
    for blows,
Like a gay young Irish gentleman, all of the present time.

Thro' Dublin then, in bang-up style, amid the jovial band,
He'd dash along twelve miles an hour, and sport his four
    in hand;
Nor were the sick or destitute ever driven from his door,
For though for fun he was inclined, his purse relieved the
    poor,
Like a fine young Irish gentleman, all of the present time.

If absentees, like this young lord, would but return once
    more,
Encourage trade of every grade, on this their native shore,
Then they would find that many a heart revived with hope
    would be,
Let Erin boast, she's like the soul, an eagle bold and free,
Like this gay young Irish gentleman, our liberties to guard.

Let every true heart then unite in this their common cause,
To help the poor, support the queen, and sanction all just
    laws;
And while these things they hope to do, may all disssen-
    sions cease, ˙
Then let our motto always be, old Erin's lasting peace,
Like this gay young Irish gentleman, who loves his native
    land.

Then here's success to this young lord, wherever he may
    be,
Let's pledge our bumpers to the brim, and drink with three
    times three;
Then when the sparkling glass goes around, I'll propose
    the toast—
Here's to him—you all know who—and may we always
    boast
Of this fine young Irish gentleman, who loves his native
    land.

THE NIGHT BEFORE LARRY WAS STRETCHED.

Written by the late J. P. Curran, Esq.

The night before Larry was stretched,
The boys they all paid him a visit,
  A bit in their sacks too they fetched,
They sweated their duds till they riz it;
  For Larry was always the lad,
When a friend was condemned to the squeezer,
  But he'd fence all the togs that he had,
To help a poor friend to the sneezer,
  And moisten his gob 'fore he died.

"I'm sorry now, Larry," says I,
"To see you in this situation;
  Pon my conscience, my lad, I don't lie,
I'd rather it had been my own station."
  "Och hone! 'tis all over," says he,
"For the neckcloth I'm forced to put on,
  And by this time to-morrow you'll see,
Your Larry will be dead as mutton,
  Because why, my dear, my courage was good."

The boys they came crowding in fast,
They drew all their stools round about him;
  Six glims round his trap-case were placed.
He could not be well waked without them;
  I axed if he were fit for to die,
Without having duly repented?
  Says Larry, "that's all in my eye.
It's only what gownsmen invented,
  To get a fat bit for themselves."

The cards being called for, they played
Till Larry found one of them cheated,
  He made a smart stroke for the head,
(The boy being easily heated),
  "Och! by the holy, you thief,
I'll scuttle your nob with my daddle,
  You cheat me because I'm in grief,

But soon I'll demolish your noddle,
    And leave you your claret to drink."

    Then in came the priest with his book,
He spoke him so smooth and so civil,
    Larry tipped him a Kilmainham look,
And pitched his big wig to the devil.
    Then stooping a little his head,
To get a sweet drop of the bottle,
    And pitiful sighing he said,
Oh, the hemp will be soon round my throttle
    And choke my poor windpipe to death.

    So moving his last words he spoke,
We all vented our tears in a shower;
    For my part, I thought my heart broke,
To see him cut down like a flower.
    On his travels we watched him next day,
Oh the hangman I thought I could kill him,
    Nor one word poor Larry did say,
Not changed till he came to King William.
    Then my dear his color turned white.

    When he came to the nubbling chit,
He was tucked up so nate and so pretty
    The rumbler jogged off from his feet,
And he died with his face to the city.
    He kicked too—but that was all pride
For soon you might see 'twas all over,
    Soon after the noose was untied,
And at dark we waked him in clover,
    And sent him to take a ground sweat.

WHAT MAN WOULD BE WITHOUT A WIFE I SHOULD LIKE TO KNOW.

Though much is said and sung about a woman's tongue,
I think that I can prove to you its merits ere it's long;

To the sex I'll tune my lays, and adore them all my
     days,
And now it's my intention for to sing in woman's
     praise;
  I'll prove a lovely woman is a man's best friend,
  Back and edge she'll stick to him till life doth end,
The man who'd single go, had better be below,
For what man would be without a woman, I would like to
     know.

                The man, &c.

If a man has got a wife, he may lead a steady life,
Although by turns the best of folks may have a little
     strife;
Woman's tongue must have its power, but her passion's
     like a shower
In April, when the rain and sunshine's all in an hour;
  A man may better let a woman have her way,
  Let her chatter, chatter, all the day;
For tho' her tongue may go in scandal to and fro,
What man would have a woman dumb, I would like to
     know.

              Tho' her tongue, &c.

At home she's man's best friend, for him she'll wash and
     mend,
And unto all his many little wants she will attend;
While a single man it's true, for himself must wash and
     stew,
Mend his clothes, wash his shirt, and Molly coddle too;
  A married man too happy can never fail,
  While a single man is like a dog without a tail;
Poor and ragged he must go, unless he'll botch and sew,
So what man would be a Molly all his life, I'd like to
     know.

             Poor and ragged, &c.

Tho' the child he'll have to nurse, yet still he may do
     worse,

Tho' when it wets him thro' and thro', perhaps 'twill make
    him curse,
It shows he is a man, and something do he can,
It proves the woman loves him, and acts a steady plan ;
  Then perhaps he'll have to drag the child about,
   And often put in his hat a dirty clout ;
Yet if he must do so, affection it does show,
And where's the man that wouldn't love his own I'd like
    to know.

                  Yet if he must, &c.

Then if his wife is gay, and wish to toy and play,
And a man that often pleased her pop into the way,
She may at him wink and leer, still her husband should
    not care,
For when she loves him dearly, if he's jealous he's a bear!
  This offence may often make them nearly fight,
  But I'm sure they will make it up that night,
For when to bed they go, they'll soon get friends, and so,
What state can equal matrimony, I would like to know.

                  For when, &c.

A horse without a fair, it is like a desert drear,
Like garden without flowers or vegetation near,
Like a tail without a head, like a bedstead without bed,
So, lads, if you're not silly, I'd have you quickly wed ;
  A single life you'll find a bitter pill,
  No one to sooth or nurse you if by and by you're ill ;
So a woman, I can show, is man's only friend below,
So what man would be without a woman, I would like to
    know.

                So a woman, &c.

THE PIPER.

From the Legend of Samuel Lover, Esq.

In the year ninety-eight when our troubles were great,
  It was treason to be a Milesian :

I can never forget the big whiskered set,
   Whom history tells us were Hessians:
In them heart-breaking times we had all kinds of crimes,
   As murdering never was riper—
On the hill of Glancree, not an acre from me,
   Lived bould Denny Byrne, the piper.

Neither wedding or wake was worth an old shake
   If Denny was not first invited,
For at emptying the kegs or squeezing the bags,
   He astonished as well as delighted:
In such times, poor Denny couldn't earn a penny—
   Martial-law had a sting like a viper—
It kept Denny within till his bones and his skin
   Were grinning through the rags on the piper.

One heavenly night as the moon shone out bright,
   As Denny stole home by Drumdhangan,
He happened to see from the branch of a tree,
   The corpse of a Hessian there hanging:
Says Denny "these rogues have fine boots, I've no brogues
   He laid on the heels such a griper,
They were so gallis tight, and he pulled with such might
   That both legs and boots came with the piper!

He tucked up the legs and he took to his pegs,
   Till he came to Tim Cavanagh's cabin,
"*Bluranages*," says Tim, "sure I can't let you in,
   You'll be shot if you stop out there rappin'.
He sent him round to the shed, where the cow was in bed,
   With a wisp he began for to wipe her,
They lay down together on the *seven foot feathers*,
   And the cow began hugging the piper.

The day light soon dawned, Denny got up and yawned,
   Then he dragged on the boots of the Hessian;
The legs, by the law, he threw them on the straw,
   And he gave them leg-bail on his mission.
When Tim's breakfast was done, he sent out his son,
   To make Denny leap like a lamp-lighter,

6

The two legs were there—he roared like a young bear,
  " *Oh daddy, de cow eat de piper !*"

"May bad luck to the *baste*, she'd a musical taste,"
  Says Tim, "to get such a *chanter*,
Here *Phadric, avic,* take this lump of a stick,
  Drive her up to Glanealy, I'll can't her."
Mrs. Cavanagh bawled—the neighbors were called,
  They began to humbug and to jib her,
To the churchyard they *walks*, with the legs in a box,
    And she crying "we'll be hanged for the piper."

The cow was then drove just a mile or two off,
  To a fair by the side of Glanealy,
And the *crathur* was sold for four guineas in gold,
  To the clerk of the parish—Jim Daly.
They went into a tent, and the luck-penny spent,
  (For the clerk was a woeful old swiper)
Who the dickens was there playing the 'rakes O'Kildare.'
  But their friend Denny Byrne, the piper!

Tim gave a *boult* like a half broken colt,
  At the piper he looked like a gommach;
Says he, "by the powers! I thought these eight hours
  You were playing in Dhrimandhu's stomach."
But Denny observed how the Hessian was served,
  So they all wished Nick's cure to the viper,
And for *gra* that they met, their whistles they wet,
  And like devils they danced round the piper.

THE DARLIN' OULD STICK.

Air—"Teddy O'Toole."

My name is bold Morgan M'Carthy, from Trim,
My relations all died, except one brother Jim,
He's gone a sojering out to *Cow Bu'l* (Cabool),
I dare say he's laid low with a *knick* in the skull;

But let him be dead or be living,
A prayer for his corpse I'll be giving,
To send him soon home or to heaven,
    For he left me this darlin' ould stick.

If that stick had a tongue, it could tell you some tales,
How it battered the countenances of the O'Neills,
It made bits of skulls fly about in the air,
And it's been the promoter of fun at each fair,
    For I swear by the toe-nail of Moses!
    It has often broke bridges of noses,
    Of the faction that dare to oppose us—
      It's the darlin' *kippeen* of a stick.

The last time I used it, 'twas at Patrick's day,
Larry Fegan and I got into a *shilley*,
We went on a spree to the fair at Athboy,
Where I danced, and when done, I kissed Kate M'Evoy,
    Then her sweetheart went out for his cousin,
    And by *Jabers!* he brought in a dozen;
    A *doldhrum* they would have knocked us in,
      If I hadn't the *taste* of a stick!

"War," was the word, when the faction came in,
And to pummice us well, they peeled off in their skin;
Like a Hercules there I stood for the attack,
And the first that came up, I sent down on his back;
    Then I shoved out the eye of Pat Clancy,
    (For he once humbugged sister Nancy),
    In the meantime poor Kate took a fancy
      To myself and a bit of a stick.

I *smathered* her sweetheart until he was black,
She then tipped me the wink—we were off in a crack—
We went to a house 'tother end of the town,
And we cheered up our spirits by letting some down.
    When I got her snug into a corner,
    And the whiskey beginning to warm her,
    She told me her sweetheart was an informer,
      Oh! 'twas then I said prayers for my stick.

We got *whiskificated* to such a degree,
For support my poor Kate had to lean against me;
I promised to see her safe to her abode,
By the *tarnal* we fell clean in the mud, on the road;
    We were roused by the magistrate's order,
    Before we could get a toe further—
    Surrounded by peelers for murther,
      Was myself and my innocent stick.

When the trial came on, Katy swore to the fact,
That before I set-to I was decently whacked,
And the judge had a little more feeling than sense
He said what I done was in my own defence;
    But one chap swore again me, named Carey,
    (Though that night he was in Tipperary)
    He'd swear—a coal-porter was a canary!
      To transport myself and my stick.

When I was acquitted I leaped from the dock,
And the gay fellows all round me did flock;
I'd a pain in my shoulder, I shook hands so often
For the boys all imagined I'd see my own coffin.
    I went and bought a gold ring, sirs,
    And Kate to the priest I did bring, sirs,
    So next night you come, I will sing, sirs,
      The adventures of me and my stick.

WIDOW MALONE.

Written by Charles Lever.

Did you hear of the Widow Malone
                 Ohone!
Who lived in the town of Athlone?
                 Ohone!
    Oh, she melted the hearts
    Of the swains in their parts,
So lovely the Widow Malone.
                 Ohone!
So lovely the Widow Malone

Of lovers she had a full score,
                    Or more,
And fortunes they all had galore,
                    In store;
    From the minister down
    To the clerk of the crown
All were courting the Widow Malone,
                    Ohone!
All were courting the Widow Malone.

But so modest was Mistress Malone,
                    'Twas known,
No one could see her alone,
                    Ohone!
    Let them ogle and sigh,
    They could ne'er catch her eye,
So bashful the Widow Malone,
                    Ohone!
So bashful the Widow Malone.

Till one Mister O'Brien, from Clare—
                    How queer!—
It's little for blushing they care
                    Down there,
    Put his arm round her waist—
    Gave ten kisses at least—
Oh, says he, you're my Molly Malone;
                    My own,
Oh, says he, you're my Molly Malone.

And the widow they all thought so shy
                    My eye!
Ne'er thought of a simper or sigh,
                    For why?
    But Lucius, says she,
    Since you've now made so free,
You may marry your Mary Malone,
                    Ohone!
You may marry your Mary Malone.

6*

There's a moral contained in my song,
    Not wrong,
And one comfort, it's not very long,
    But strong—
  If for widows you die,
  Learn to kiss not to sigh,
For they're all like sweet Mistress Malone,
    Ohone!
Oh, they're all like sweet Mistress Malone.

THE WAKE OF TEDDY THE TILER.

From Dublin town, the other night,
A courier came with all his might,
To tell us of a jolly fight,
  At the wake of Teddy the Tiler.
Poor Teddy was a mason's man,
His face was like a warming pan,
And every night he had a plan,
To go and visit Judy Gann,
At the cabin among all the bogs,
Where Patrick banished toads and frogs,
Grunting and squeaking were the hogs,
  At the wake of Teddy the Tiler.
  Phillalloo, hubbaboo, whack, hurra!
  Tear away, fight away, Erin go bragh,
  There was a grand potato war,
  At the wake of Teddy the Tiler.

One morning Teddy went with tiles,
To tile the house of Paddy Miles,
Who won Miss Judy Gann with smiles,
  For the wake of Teddy the Tiler.
As Teddy up the ladder trod,
Wid mortar in Pat Murphy's hod,
Miss Judy Gann began to nod,
  And called him one of the awkward squad;
She then kissed Paddy Miles, and found
Poor Teddy lifeless on the ground,

To a coroner's inquest soon were bound,
  To the wake of Teddy the Tiler,
                Phillilloo, &c

On a shutter home they carried Ted,
And laid him out upon his bed,
A large red night-cap topped his head,
  At the wake of Teddy the Tiler.
A howling then they did agree,
That Teddy died felo—de—see,
'Cause Judy Gann, false-hearted she,
Kiss'd Paddy Miles upon his knee.
The female ladies then began
To black the eyes of Judy Gann,
And swore she shouldn't boast a man,
  At the wake of Teddy the Tiler.
                Phillilloo, &c

To love and whiskey some would yield,
While others for a row soon peeled,
And marched off to a potato field,
  At the wake of Teddy the Tiler.
Potatoes in the field that grew,
To make Paddy's Irish stew,
Up in the air some thousands flew,
Like shots and balls at Waterloo;
A kidney tater—such a size!
Met Paddy Flinn between the eyes,
And sent him into one of his sties,
  At the wake of Teddy the Tiler.
                Phillilloo, &c

While they were fighting all that day,
A burker stole poor Ted away,
And then there was the d——l to pay,
  At the wake of Teddy the Tiler.
To find poor Ted some did engage,
Some put each other in a rage,
Police were sent to assuage,
And some were shoved into a cage;

Miss Judy Gann ran home to roost,
But cracked her head against a post,
And so the fool gave up the ghost,
   At the wake of Teddy the Tiler.
                Philliloo, &c,

THE LOVES OF JUDY ROONEY AND LOONEY CONNOR.

AIR.—" Nancy Dawson."

Och! Judy Rooney, nate and tight,
'Twas she first gave my heart delight,
In bed I staid awake all night,
   A thinking of her beauty.

For oh! her eyes such conquest draws,
That she has gained the world's applause,
And Judy plays with hearts like straws;
   With which, a knot but few tie!

Resolved to speak my mind one day,
I sought Miss Rooney where she lay,
Reclining on a cock of hay,
   Her cheeks so rosy red, gra.

Says I, och! Judy give relief,
For Love, that universal thief,
Has nearly kilt myself with grief,
   Unless with me you'll wed, gra.

The livelong night the ne'er a wink,
I get, but still of you I think,—
Since sorrow's dry, myself must drink,
   Then bid not Looney part you

For since my heart to you has flown,
My night-cap it has useless grown,
So e'en take that, they're both your own.
   My night-cap and my heart too.

With that the soul, she smiled to hear,
Her lovely self, to me was dear,
And Judy's smiles brought hope to cheer
    The faithful heart of Looney.

Upon the hay I bent my knee,
Your night-cap you may keep, says she,
But t'other trifle leave with me,
    Your own true Judy Rooney.

So then I threw my cap at care,
And no one but ourselves being there,
I just made bold to kiss the fair,
    While blushes crowded on her.

With down-cast eyes she sighed a power,
She owned—of youths I was the flower,
And Judy Rooney from that hour
    Is Mrs. Looney Connor.

KATTY AVOURNEEN.

'Twas a cold winter's night, and the tempest was snarling,
  The snow like a sheet covered cabin and sty;
When Barney flew over the hills to his darling,
  And tapped at the window, where Katty did lie,
"Arrah jewil," says he, "are you sleepin' or wakin',
  It's a bitter cold night, and my coat it is thin;
The storm is a brewin', the frost is a bakin',
  O, Katty Avourneen, you must let me in."

"Ah, then, Barney," says Kate, and she spoke through the
    window,
  "How could you be takin' us out of our bed?
To come at this time it's a shame and a sin, too,
  It's whiskey, not love, has got into your head.
If your heart it was true, of my fame you'd be tender;
  Consider the time, and there's nobody in?

What has a poor girl but her name to defend her,
  No, Barney Avourneen, I won't let you in!"

" A-cush-la," says he, "it's my eye is a fountain,
  That weeps for the wrong I might lay at your door,
Your name is more white than the snow on the mountain,
  And Barney will die to preserve it as pure.
I'll go to my home, though the winter winds face me,
  I'll whistle them off, for I'm happy within,
And the words of my Katty shall comfort and bless me—
  'No, Barney Avourneen, I won't let you in.' "

SHELAH O'NEAL.

When first I began for to sigh and to woo her,
  Of many fine things I did say a great deal ;
But, above all the rest, that which pleased her the
      best,
Was—Och, will you marry me, Shelah O'Neal?
        My point I soon carried,
        For straight we were married,
Then the weight of my burden I soon 'gan to feel,
        For she scolded, she fisted,
        O, then I enlisted,
Left Ireland, and whiskey, and Shelah O'Neal.

Then tired, and dull-hearted, O, then I deserted,
  I fled into regions far-distant from home,
To Frederick's army, where none e'er could harm me,
  Save Shelah herself in the shape of a bomb.
        I fought every battle,
        Where cannons did rattle,
Felt sharp shot, alas! and the sharp-pointed steel,
        But in all my wars round,
        Thank my stars, I ne'er found
Aught so sharp as the tongue of curs'd Shelah O'Neal.

IRISH HEARTS FOR THE LADIES.

One day Madam Nature was busy,
   Bright Venus beside her was seated,
She looked till her head was quite dizzy,
   She long'd till the job was completed;
I'm making a heart, cried the goddess,
   For love and its joys, all my trade is,
Not a heart for a stays, or a boddice,
   But an Irishman's heart for the ladies.

She bound it all round with good nature;
   'Twas tender and soft as the dove, sir;
'Twas sprinkled with drops of the creature;
   'Twas stuffed too with large lumps of love, sir!
'Twas pure as the streams of the Shannon,
   As warm too as roasted potatoes,
And just like a ball from a cannon,
   Is an Irishman's heart for the ladies.

Then speak, ye deluders so pretty,
   Your own silver tongues tell the story,
That Irishmen melt you to pity,
   For they are the boys that adore ye;
In love and in war we're so frisky,
   Nor of French, Dutch, or devils, afraid is,
We've lips for our girls and our whiskey,
   And tight Irish hearts for the ladies.

GOOD MORROW TO YOUR NIGHTCAP

Dear Kathleen, you, no doubt,
   Find sleep how very sweet 'tis;
Dogs bark, and cocks crowed out,
   You never dream how late 'tis.
This morning gay, I post away,
To have with you a bit of play,

On two legs rid along, to bid
Good-morrow to your nightcap.

Last night, a little bowsy,
  With whiskey, ale, and cider,
I asked young Betty Blowsy
  To let me sit beside her.
Her anger rose, as sour as sloes,
The little gipsy cocked her nose,
  So here I've rid along, to bid
Good-morrow to your nightcap.

THE END

THE FLORENCES' IRISH BOY AND YANKEE GIRL SONGSTER.

CONTENTS :

Copies mailed to any address in the United States, free of postage, upon receipt of ten cents.

------ ◆ ------

THE LOVE AND SENTIMENTAL SONGSTER.

CONTENTS :

Copies mailed to any address in the United States, free of postage, upon the receipt of ten cents.

---◆---

THE CHARLEY O'MALLEY IRISH SONGSTER.

CONTENTS:

Copies mailed to any address in the United States, free of postage, upon receipt of ten cents.

TONY PASTOR'S COMIC SONGSTER.

CONTENTS:

A Big thing on Ice.
A Parody, (comic recitation).
A Sweetener for the Ladies.
Be Sure a Thing will Pay.
Billy, I Have Missed You.
Could'nt Stand the Press.
Don't Think Much of You.
Flying Your Kite too High.
Folks that Put on Airs.
Good Advice.
Happy Hezekiah.
Happy Land of Canaan.
I Can't See It.
Joe Bowers.
Lather and Shave.
Merry Month of May.
My Mary has the Longest Nose.
Nick, Not at Home.
Ould Irish Stew.
One Good Turn Deserves Another.
Played Out.
Sound on the Goose.
Strike while the Iron's Hot.
Something New to Wear.
Sammy Slap, the Bill-Sticker.

The Clown's Consolations to Disconsolate People.
The Age of Machinery.
The 'Orrible Tale.
The Goose Hangs High.
The Tickler.
The Ragged Coat.
The Yankee Quilting Party.
The Goot Lager Beer.
The Lazy Club.
The Farmer's Alphabet.
The "Rights of Man."
The Widow Wagtail.
The Bachelor's Dream.
The Obstinate Man.
The Traveler, (a comic recitation).
Think of your Head in the Morning.
Tuscaloosa Sam.
Unhappy Jeremiah.
Umbrella Courtship.
Wonder of the Age.
Whole Hog or None.
What will Mrs. Grundy Say?

Copies mailed to any address in the United States, free of postage, upon receipt of ten cents.

THE CAMP-FIRE SONG BOOK.

A collection of Jolly, Patriotic, Convivial, and National Songs, embracing all the Popular Camp and Marching Songs, as sung by our Army.

CONTENTS:

A Big Thing Coming.
Abraham's Daughter.
A Good Time Coming, Boys.
A Glass is Good.
America.
Annie Laurie.
Auld Lang Syne.
A Yankee Ship and a Yankee Crew.
Benny Havens.
Bully for Us.
Camp War Song.
Columbia, the Gem of the Ocean.
Come, Landlords, Fill.
Come, Raise the Banner High.
Corporal Kelly.
Dixie of Our Union.
Dixie of the Michigan Boys.
Drink it Down.
Free and Easy Still.

Gay and Happy.
God Save our Native Land.
Hail Columbia.
Happy Land of Canaan.
Home Again.
Home, Sweet Home.
How are You, Johnny Bull?
Hurrah for the Union.
I Love a Sixpence.
Jeff Davis; or, the King of the Southern Dominions.
Jonathan to John.
Let Cowards Shirk their Duty.
Little Rhode Island.
My Love, he is a Zou-zu.
My Country, 'tis of Thee I Sing.
Our Country's Flag.
Our Father Land.
Our Flag is There.
Our German Volunteers.

All the above Songs go to Popular and well-known tunes, so that they can easily be sung. Copies mailed to any address in the United States, free of postage, upon receipt of ten cents.

THE SHAMROCK; OR, SONGS OF OLD IRELAND.

CONTENTS:

Copies mailed to any address in the United States, free of postage, upon receipt of ten cents.

FRED MAY'S COMIC IRISH SONGSTER.

CONTENTS:

Copies mailed to any address in the United States, free of postage, upon receipt of ten cents.

WOOD'S MINSTREL SONG BOOK.

CONTENTS:

Copies mailed to any address in the United States, free of postage, on receipt of ten cents.

THE FRISKY IRISH SONGSTER.

CONTENTS:

An Irishman's Excuse for a Fight; or, Thread on the Tail of my Coat.
A Tight Irish Heart for the Ladies
Ballinamana Oro.
Barrel of Pork.
Batch of Cakes.
Biddy Maguire of Ballinaclash.
Bryan O'Lynn.
Cruiskeen Lawn.
Dolly Dunn of Donnybrook.
Don't You Think She Did.
Friend, by my Sowl, I'll Whisky Drink.
Gaffer Gray.
Going Home with the Milk in the Morning.
Handy Andy.
Hoppy Hoolahan's Lament on the Death of His Duck.
Horticultural Wife.
Jeff Davis.
Larry McHale.
Murrough O'Monahan.
Murthough Delany's Birth.
Nell Flaugherty's Drake.
Paddy Goshlow.
Paddy's Grave.
Pat and the Priest.
Petticoat Lane.
Robinson Crusoe.
Sheelah O'Neal.
Soldier's Dream.
Sprig of Shillelah.
Summer Hill Courtship.
The Anchor's Weighed.
The Bells of Shandon.
The Freemason.
The Great, Big, Ugly Irishman.
The Guager's Slip.
The Humors of Passage.
The Hungry Army.
The Jolly Beggar.
The Land of Shillelah.
The Man in the Moon.
The Miller's Song.
The Muleteer.
The New York Volunteer.
The Pirate Crew.
The Stars and Stripes.
The Wedding of Ballyporeen.
The Widow that Keeps the Cock Inn.
The Wild Irishman.
There's Room for All.
Useful Knowledge.
What an Illigant Life a Friar Leads
Young Volunteer.

Copies mailed to any address in the United States, free of postage, upon receipt of ten cents.

GUS SHAW'S COMIC SONG BOOK.

CONTENTS:

Alonzo, the Brave.
Shells of Oysters.
The Bill-Poster.
Mr. and Mrs. Snibbs.
Nora Daley.
St. Patrick's Birth-Day.
The Female Smuggler.
The Lively Flea.
Sights for a Father.
Nepoletaine.
My Mother was a True Born Irishman.
Paper Song.
Mr. and Mrs. Bone.
Robin Ruff and Gaffer Green.
Root, Hog, or Die.
Rat Catcher's Daughter.
Larboard Watch.
Larry O'Brien.
The Irishman's Shanty.
New York in Slices.
Hamlet—A Tragedy.
Nonsense.
Bumper of Lager.
Brogue and Blarney.
My Mary's Nose.
Fair of Clogheen.
Billy Nutts, the Poet.
In the Days when I was Hard Up.
The Irish Jaunting Car.
Wooden Leg Sailor.
The Sicilian Maid.

Copies mailed to any address in the United States, free of postage, upon receipt of ten cents.

WOOD'S NEW PLANTATION MELODIES.

CONTENTS :

Belle of Alabama.
Belle of Baltimore.
Belle of Tennessee.
Come, Darkies, Listen to Dis Song.
Chorus from Somnambula.
Dandy Broadway Swell.
Dearest Mae.
De Corn Top Blossom.
De Purty Yellow Gal am a Warning.
De Skeeters do Bite.
De Yellow Gal wid a Bloomer on.
De York River by Steamboat.
Eighty-one Conundrums and Jokes
Eph Horn's Celebrated Story of the Misfortunes of his Lady Love.
Ephriam's Lament.
False Hearted Clementina.
Fare Thee Well, Kitty Dear.
Gal wid de Blue Dress on.
Gwine to Run all Night.
Hark, I Hear an Angel Sing.
Have a Little Dance.
Hoe On.
Hop Light, Loo.
Jordan is a Hard Road to Travel.
Julia is a Beauty.

Life by the Galley Fire.
Lubly Rosa.
Louisiana Bell.
Mary Blane.
New Darkey Medley.
Oh! Silber Shining Moon.
Oh, Lud Gals.
Oh, Susannah.
Parody on the Lady of Lyons.
Pirate's Chorus.
Ride on, Darkies.
Rosa Lee.
Sally Weaver.
See! Sir, See!
Somebody's in de House wid Susey.
Swash Shaw, Hands Across.
Sweep oh! Sweep oh!
The Celebrated Black Shaker Song.
The Merry Sleigh Bells.
The Little Nigger Sweep.
The Possum's Retreat.
Tread Lightly.
Uncle Ned.
Way Down on the Old Pee Dee.
Whar is de Spot.
Yes, 'Tis True, Thy Katy Now is Sleeping.

Copies mailed to any address in the United States, free of postage, on receipt of ten cents.

HARRISON'S COMIC SONGSTER.

CONTENTS :

Bachelor Management.
Courting Two Sweethearts at Once.
Did You Ever?
Doctor Brown.
Hymen's Court.
If it Wasn't for Rain.
If You Think You've Many Friends.
I'm a Constable.
I'm a 'Prentice Boy.
Joys of Winter.
Mankind are all Birds.
Miseries of an Omnibus.
One Suit Between Two.

Provided You've Money to Pay for it.
Raspberry Wine.
Rural Felicity.
Steamboat Excursion.
The Boarding-house Keeper's Keeper's Miseries.
The Doctor's Boy.
The Lazy Family.
The Little Man.
The Model Artist.
The Very Singular Man.
Very Polite of Her.
Whiskers.

Copies mailed to any address in the United States, free of postage, upon receipt of ten cents.

TONY PASTOR'S UNION SONG BOOK.

CONTENTS:

Copies mailed to any address in the United States, free of postage upon receipt of ten cents.

BOB HART'S PLANTATION SONGSTER.

CONTENTS:

Copies mailed to any address in the United States, free of postage, upon receipt of ten cents.

Popular Books sent Free of Postage at the prices annexed.

The Sociable; *or, One Thousand and One Home Amusements.* Containing Acting Proverbs, Dramatic Charades, Acting Charades, Tableaux Vivants, Parlor Games, and Parlor Magic, and a choice collection of Puzzles, &c., illustrated with nearly 300 Engravings and Diagrams, the whole being a fund of never-ending entertainment. By the Author of the "Magician's Own Book." Nearly 400 pages, 12mo., cloth, gilt side stamp................. ...Price $1.00.

Inquire Within *for Anything You Want to Know; or, Over* 3,700 *Facts for the People.* Illustrated, 436 large pages...Price $1.00.

"Inquire Within" is one of the most valuable and extraordinary volumes ever presented to the American public, and embodies nearly 4,000 facts, in most of which any person living will find instruction, aid, and entertainment. It contains so many valuable and useful recipes, that an enumeration of them requires *seventy-two columns of fine type for the Index.*

The Corner Cupboard; *or, Facts for Everybody.* By the Author of "Inquire Within," "The Reason Why," &c. Large 12mo., 400 pages, cloth, gilt side and back. Illustrated with over 1000 Engravings.
Price $1.00.

The Reason Why: *General Science.* A careful collection of some thousands of reasons for things, which, though generally known, are imperfectly understood. By the Author of "Inquire Within." A handsome 12mo. volume of 356 pages, cloth, gilt, and embellished with a large number of wood-cuts.................Price $1.00.

The Biblical Reason Why: A Hand-Book for Biblical Students, and a Guide to Family Scripture Readings. By the Author of "Inquire Within, &c. Beautifully illustrated, large 12mo. cloth, gilt side and back..Price $1.00.

The Reason Why: *Natural History.* By the Author of "Inquire Within," "The Biblical Reason Why," &c. 12mo. cloth, gilt side and back. Giving Reasons for hundreds of interesting facts in Natural History...Price $1.00.

10,000 Wonderful Things. Comprising the Marvellous and Rare, Odd, Curious, Quaint, Eccentric, and Extraordinary, in all Ages and Nations, in Art, Nature, and Science, including many Wonders of the world, enriched with Hundreds of Authentic Illustrations. 12mo. cloth, gilt side and back ....Price $1.00.

That's It; *or, Plain Teaching* By the Author of "Inquire Within," "The Reason Why." &c. Illustrated with over 1,200 Wood-cuts. 12mo. cloth, gilt side and back...................Price $1.00.

The Lady's Manual of Fancy Work A Complete Instructor in every variety of Ornamental Needle-Work; including Shading and Coloring, Printer's Marks, Explanatory Terms, &c., &c. The Whole being a Complete Lexicon of Fancy Work. By Mrs. PULLAN, Director of the Work-table of Frank Leslie's Magazine, &c., &c. Illustrated with over 300 Engravings, by the best Artists, with eight large pattern plates, elegantly printed in colors on tinted paper. Large 8vo., beautifully bound in fine cloth, with gilt side and back stamp.
Price $1.25.

Popular Books sent Free of Postage at the prices annexed.

The Secret Out: *or, One Thousand Tricks with Cards and other Recreations.* Illustrated with over Three Hundred Engravings. A book which explains all the Tricks and Deceptions with Playing Cards ever known or invented, and gives, besides, a great many new and interesting ones—the whole being described so accurately and carefully, with engravings to illustrate them, that anybody can easily learn how to practice these Tricks. This work also contains 240 of the best Tricks in Legerdemain, in addition to the card tricks. 12mo, 400 pages, bound in cloth, with gilt side and back................Price $1 00.

The Art of Dancing, Containing the Figures, Music, and necessary instruction for all Modern Approved Dances. Also, Hints on Etiquette and the Ethics of Politeness. By EDWARD FERRERO, Professor of Dancing, &c. A large bound book, full of Engravings and Music to illustrate it..Price $1.00.

The Dictionary of Love. Containing a Definition of all the terms used in Courtship, with rare quotations from Poets of all Nations, together with specimens of curious Model Love Letters, and many other interesting matters appertaining to Love, never before published. 12mo, cloth, gilt side and back............................Price $1.00.

The Magician's Own Book. Being a Hand-Book of Parlor Magic, and containing several hundred amusing Magical, Magnetical, Electrical, and Chemical Experiments, Astonishing Transmutations, Wonderful Sleight-of-Hand and Card Tricks, Curious and Perplexing Puzzles, Quaint Questions in Numbers, &c., together with all the most noted Tricks of Modern Performers. Illustrated with over 500 Wood Engravings. 12mo, cloth, gilt side and back stamp, 400 pages.
Price $1.00.

The Book of 1,000 Tales and Amusing Adventures. Containing over 300 Engravings, and 450 pages. This is a magnificent book, and is crammed full of narratives and adventures........Price $1.00.

The Bordeaux Wine and Liquor Dealer's Guide; *or, How to Manufacture and Adulterate Liquors*. By a practical Liquor Manufacturer. 12mo, cloth...Price $1.00.

In this work, *not one* article in the smallest degree approximating to a poison is recommended, and yet the book teaches how Cognac Brandy, Scotch and Irish Whiskey, Foreign and Domestic Rum, all kinds of Wines, Cordials, &c., from the choicest to the commonest, can be imitated to that perfection that the best judges cannot detect the method of manufacture, even by chemical tests of the severest character.

Ladies' Guide to Crochet. By Mrs. ANN S. STEPHENS. Copiously illustrated with original and very choice designs in Crochet, etc., printed in colors, separate from the letter press, on tinted paper. Also with numerous wood-cuts, printed with the letter press, explanatory of terms, etc. Oblong, pp 117, beautifully bound in extra cloth, gilt. This is by far the best work on the subject of Crochet ever published.
Price 75 cts.

Arts of Beauty ; *or, Secrets of a Lady's Toilet.* With Hints to Gentlemen on the Art of Fascinating. By Madame LOLA MONTEZ, Countess of Landsfeldt. Cloth, gilt side. This book contains an account, in detail, of all the arts employed by the fashionable ladies of all the chief cities of Europe, for the purpose of developing and preserving their charms .... Price 50 cts.

Popular Books sent Free of Postage at the prices annexed.

Every Woman Her Own Lawyer. A private Guide in all matters of Law, of essential interest to Women, and by the aid of which every Female may, in whatever situation, understand her legal course and redress, and be her own Legal Adviser. By GEORGE BISHOP. Large 12mo, nearly 400 pages, bound in half leather. This book should be in the hands of every woman, young or old, married or single, in the United States..Price $1 00.

Richardson's Monitor of Free-Masonry: A Complete Guide to the various Ceremonies and Routine in Free-Masons' Lodges, Chapters, Encampments, Hierarchies, &c., &c., in all the Degrees, whether Modern, Ancient, Ineffable, Philosophical, or Historical. Containing, also, the Signs, Tokens, Grips, Pass-words, Decorations, Drapery, Dress, Regalia, and Jewels, in each Degree. Profusely illustrated with Explanatory Engravings, Plans of the Interior of Lodges, &c, By JABEZ RICHARDSON, A. M. A book of 185 pages.
Bound in paper covers ....Price 30 cts.
Bound and gilt ....Price 50 cts.
This is the only book ever written which gives a detailed description of all the doings inside a Masonic meeting.

The Manufacture of Liquors, Wines, and Cordials. Without the aid of Distillation; also, the Manufacture of Effervescing Beverages, and Syrups, Vinegar, and Bitters. Prepared and arranged expressly for the Trade. By PIERRE LACOUR. Procure a copy of "Lacour on the Manufacture of Liquors," or if you do not wish to purchase, look through the book for a few moments as a matter of curiosity. Physicians' and Druggists' pharmaceutical knowledge cannot be complete without a copy of this work. 12mo, cloth.............Price $1.50.

Mrs. Partington's Carpet-Bag of Fun. A Collection of over one thousand of the most comical stories, amusing adventures, side-splitting jokes, check-extending poetry, funny conundrums, QUEER SAYINGS OF MRS. PARTINGTON, heart-rending puns, witty repartees, etc., etc. The whole illustrated by about 150 comic wood cuts.
12mo, 300 pages, cloth, gilt............................Price 75 cts.
Ornamented paper covers...............................Price 50 cts.

Sam Slick in Search of a Wife. 12mo, paper..........Price 50 cts.
Cloth..Price 75 cts.
Everybody has heard of "Sam Slick, the Clockmaker," and he has given his opinion on almost everything.

Sam Slick's Nature and Human Nature. Large 12mo.
Paper..Price 50 cts.
Cloth...Price 75 cts.

The Attachee: or, Sam Slick in England. Large 12mo.
Paper ....Price 50 cts.
Cloth...Price 75 cts.

Sam Slick's Sayings and Doings. Paper.............Price 50 cts.
Cloth...Price 75 cts

The Game of Draughts, or Checkers, Simplified and Explained. With Practical Diagrams and Illustrations, together with a Checker board, numbered and printed in red. Containing the Eighteen Standard Games, with over 200 of the best variations, selected from the various authors, together with many original ones never before published. By D. SCATTERGOOD. Bound in cloth, with flexible cover..Price 38 cts.

Popular Books sent Free of Postage at the prices annexed.

Pettengill's Perfect Fortune-Teller and Dream-Book: *or, The Art of Discerning Future Events,* as practiced by Modern Seers and Astrologers—being also a Key to the Hidden Mysteries of the Middle Ages. To which is added Curious and Amusing Charms, Invocations, Signs, &c., &c. By PELETIAH PETTENGILL, Philom. A book of 141 pages, bound in boards, with cloth back ....**Price 25 cts.**

Courtship Made Easy; *or, The Art of Making Love fully Explained.* Containing full and minute directions for conducting a Courtship with Ladies of every age and position in society, and valuable information for persons who desire to enter the marriage state. Also, Forms of Love Letters to be used on certain occasions. 64 pp. **Price 12 cts.**

Chesterfield's Art of Letter-writing Simplified. A Guide to Friendly, Affectionate, Polite, and Business Correspondence....**Price 12 cts.**

Containing a large collection of the most valuable information relative to the Art of Letter-Writing, with clear and complete instructions how to begin and end correspondence, Rules for Punctuation and Spelling, &c., together with numerous examples of Letters and Notes on every subject of Epistolary Intercourse, with several Important Hints on Love Letters.

Knowlson's Farrier, *and Complete Horse Doctor.* We have printed a new and revised edition of this celebrated book, which contains Knowlsons famous Recipe for the cure of Spavin, and other new matter. It is positively the best book of the kind ever written. We sell it cheap because of the immense demand for it. The farmers and horse-keepers like it because it gives them plain common-sense directions how to manage their horses. We sell our new edition (64 pages, 18mo,) cheap ....**Price 12 cts.**

The Art of Conversation: With Remarks on Fashion and Address. By MRS. MABERLY. This is the best book on the subject ever published. It contains nothing that is verbose or difficult to understand, but all the instructions and rules for conversation are given in a plain and common-sense manner, so that any one, however dull, can easily comprehend them. 64 pages octavo, large...........**Price 25 cts.**

Horse-Taming by a New Method, *as Practiced by J. S. Rarey.* A New and Improved Edition, containing Mr. Rarey's whole Secret of Subduing and Breaking Vicious Horses, together with his Improved Plan of Managing Young Colts, and Breaking them to the Saddle, the Harness, and the Sulkey—with ten engravings illustrating the process. Every person who keeps a horse should buy this book. It costs but a trifle, and you will positively find it an excellent guide in the management of that noble animal. This is a very handsome book of 64 pages ....**Price 12 cts.**

The Game of Whist: Rules, Directions and Maxims to be observed in playing it. Containing also Primary Rules for Beginners, Explanations and Directions for Old Players, and the Laws of the Game. Compiled from Hoyle and Matthews. Also, Loo, Euchre, and Poker, as now generally played—with an explanation of Marked Cards, &c., &c....................................**Price 12 cts.**

The Young Bride's Book: An Epitome of the Social and Domestic Duties of Woman, as the Wife and the Mother. By ARTHUR FREELING. This is one of the best and most useful books ever issued in the cheap form. It is printed in clear and beautiful type, and on fine paper....................................**Price 12 cts.**

Popular Books sent Free of Postage at the prices annexed.

The Ladies' Love Oracle; *or, Counsellor to the Fair Sex.* Being a complete Fortune Teller and Interpreter to all questions upon the different events and situations of life, but more especially relating to all circumstances connected with Love, Courtship, and Marriage. By Madame Le Marchand. Beautifully illustrated cover, printed in colors..Price 25 cts.

The Laws of Love. A complete Code of Gallantry. 12 mo. Paper...Price 25 cts.

Containing concise rules for the conduct of Courtship through its entire progress, aphorisms of love, rules for telling the characters and dispositions of women, remedies for love, and an Epistolary Code.

Gamblers' Tricks with Cards Exposed and Explained. By J. H. Green, Reformed Gambler. 12mo, paper..........Price 25 cts.

This work contains one hundred tricks with cards, explained, and shows the numerous cheats which Gamblers practice upon their unwary dupes.

How to Win and How to Woo. Containing Rules for the Etiquette of Courtship, with directions showing how to win the favor of Ladies, how to begin and end a Courtship, and how Love Letters should be written..Price 12 cts.

Bridal Etiquette. A Sensible Guide to the Etiquette and Observances of the Marriage Ceremonies; containing complete directions for Bridal Receptions, and the necessary rules for bridesmaids, groomsmen sending cards, &c., &c..............................Price 12 cts.

How to Behave; *or, The Spirit of Etiquette.* A Complete Guide to Polite Society, for Ladies and Gentlemen; containing rules for good behavior at the dinner table, in the parlor, and in the street; with important hints on introduction, conversation, &c....Price 12 cts.

The Everlasting Fortune-Teller and Magnetic Dream-Book. Containing the science of foretelling events by the Signs of the Zodiac, Lists of Lucky and Unlucky Days, with Presages drawn therefrom; the science of Foretelling Events by cards, dice, &c...Price 25 cts.

Morgan's Free-Masonry Exposed and Explained. Showing the Origin, History, and Nature of Masonry; its Effects on the Government and the Christian Religion; and containing a Key to all the Degrees of Free-Masonry; giving a clear and correct view of the manner of Conferring the Different Degrees, as practiced in all Lodges throughout the Globe ....Price 25 cts.

How to Dress with Taste; Containing hints on the harmony of colors, the theory of contrast, the complexion, shape or hight, **Price 12 cts.**

Mind Your Stops: Punctuation made plain, and Composition simplified for Readers, Writers and Talkers.............Price 12 cts.

This little book is worth ten times the price asked for it, and will teach accurately in everything, from the diction of a friendly letter to the composition of a learned treatise.

Hard Words Made Easy; Rules for Pronunciation and Accent; with instructions how to pronounce French, Italian, German, Russian, Danish, Dutch, Swedish, Norwegian, and other foreign names. A capital work ....Price 12 cts.

Popular Books sent Free of Postage at the prices annexed.

Courteney's Dictionary of Abbreviations; Literary, Scientific, Commercial, Ecclesiastical, Military, Naval, Legal and Medical. A book of reference—3,000 abbreviations—for the solution of all literary mysteries. By EDWARD S. C. COURTENEY, Esq. This is a very useful book. Everybody should get a copy..........Price 12 cts.

Blunders in Behavior Corrected....................Price 12 cts.
A concise code of deportment for both sexes. "It will polish and refine either sex, and is Chesterfield superseded.—*Home Companion.*

Five Hundred French Phrases. Adapted for those who aspire to speak and write French correctly.............................Price 12 cts.

How to detect Adulteration in our Daily Food and Drink. A complete analysis of the frauds and deceptions practiced upon articles of consumption, by storekeepers and manufacturers; with full directions to detect genuine from spurious, by simple and inexpensive means..Price 12 cts.

The Young Housekeeper's Book; or, *How to have a Good Living upon a Small Income*.............................Price 12 cts.

How to be Healthy: Being a complete Guide to Long Life. By a Retired Physician.................................Price 12 cts.

How to Cut and Contrive Children's Clothes at a Small Cost. With numerous explanatory engravings....................Price 12 cts.

How to Talk and Debate; or, *Fluency of Speech Attained without the Sacrifice of Elegance and Sense.*........................Price 12 cts.

How to Manage Children.........................Price 12 cts.

The Great Wizard of the North's Hand-Book of Natural Magic. Being a series of the newest Tricks of Deception, arranged for Amateurs and Lovers of the Art. By Professor J. H. ANDERSON, the Great Wizard of the North.......................Price 25 cts.

Broad Grins of the Laughing Philosopher. Being a Collection of Funny Jokes, Droll Incidents, and Ludicrous Pictures, that will make you laugh out loud! By PICKLE THE YOUNGER, otherwise called "Little Pickle."................................Price 12 cts.

The Plate of Chowder: *A Dish for Funny Fellows.* Appropriately illustrated with 100 Comic Engravings. By the Author of "Mrs. Partington's Carpet-Bag of Fun." 12mo, paper cover....Price 25 cts.

Deacon Doolittle's Drolleries. A Collection of Funny and Laughable Stories told by the Deacon, in which he had either acted a part or taken much interest in. This book is got up especially for the benefit of thin and spare people—or for that class of mankind whom it would benefit to "Laugh and Grow Fat." It contains some thirty or forty of the best stories ever invented, full of droll and laughable incidents, calculated to drive away the blues, and to make one in good humor with all mankind......................................Price 12 cts.

The Laughable Adventures of Messrs. Brown, Jones, & Robinson, showing where they went, and how they went; what they did, and how they did it. With nearly two hundred most thrillingly-comic engravings...............................Price 25 cts.

Popular Books sent Free of Postage at the Prices annexed.

Fontaine's Golden Wheel Dream-Book and Fortune-Teller. By FELIX FONTAINE, Fortune-Teller and Astrologer. Being the most complete book on Fortune-Telling and Interpreting Dreams ever printed. Each Dream has the LUCKY NUMBER which the Dream signifies attached to it, and those who wish to purchase Lottery Tickets will do well to consult them. This book also informs you how to TELL FORTUNES with the *Golden Wheel*, with *Cards, Dice*, and *Dominoes;* how to tell future events by Psalmistry on the lines of the hands, by moles on the body, by the face, nails, and shape of the head; how to find where to dig for water, coal, and all kinds of metals, with the celebrated DIVINING ROD; Charms to make your Sweetheart love you, to make your Lover pop the question; together with Twenty Ways of Telling Fortunes on New Year's Eve. This book contains 144 pages, and is bound in pasteboard sides with cloth back. It is illustrated with numerous Engravings, showing how to hold the Divining Rod, how to lay out Cards when you Tell Fortunes, how to tell the names of your intended Wife or Husband by the charm of the Key and Book, etc. This book also contains a large Colored Lithographic Engraving of the *Golden Wheel*, which folds up. It is the cheapest on our list------------------**Price 25 cts.**

Chesterfield's Letter-Writer and Complete Book of Etiquette; or, *Concise Systematic Directions for Arranging and Writing Letters.* Also, Model Correspondence in Friendship and Business, and a great variety of Model Love Letters. If any lady or gentleman desires to know how to *begin* a Love Correspondence, this is just the book they want. If they wish to speak their minds to a tardy, a bashful, or a careless or indifferent lover, or sweetheart, this book tells exactly how it should be done. This work is also a Complete Book of Etiquette. You will find more real information in this book than in half-a-dozen volumes of the more expensive ones. It is emphatically a book for the million, and one which every young person should have. As it contains Etiquette for Ladies, as well as for Gentlemen—Etiquette of Courtship and Marriage—Etiquette for writing Love Letters, and all that sort of thing, it is an appropriate book to present to a lady. This book contains 136 pages, and is bound in pasteboard sides, with cloth back------------------**Price 25 cts.**

Le Marchand's Fortune-Teller and Dream-Book. A complete interpretation to all questions upon the different events and situations of life; but more especially relating to *Love, Courtship and Marriage.* Containing the significations of all the various Dreams, together with numerous other methods of foretelling future events. By MADAM LE MARCHAND, the celebrated Parisian Fortune-Teller------------------**Price 25 cts.**

100 Tricks With Cards. J. H. Green, the Reformed Gambler, has just authorized the publication of a new edition of his book entitled, "Gamblers' Tricks with Cards Exposed and Explained." This is a book of 96 pages, and it exposes and explains all the mysteries of the Gambling Tables. It is interesting not only to those who play, but to those who do not. Old Players will get some new ideas from this curious book------------------**Price 25 cts.**

Laughing Gas. An Encyclopædia of Wit, Wisdom, and Wind. By SAM SLICK, Jr. Comically illustrated with 100 original and laughable Engravings, and nearly 500 side-extending Jokes, and other things to get fat on; and the best of it is, that every thing about the book is new and fresh—all new—new designs, new stories, new type —no comic almanac stuff. It will be found a complete antidote to "hard times"------------------**Price 25 cts.**

Send cash orders to **Dick & Fitzgerald, 18 Ann St., N. Y.**

TONY PASTOR'S UNION SONG BOOK.

CONTENTS:

Copies mailed to any address in the United States, free of postage upon receipt of ten cents.

BOB HART'S PLANTATION SONGSTER.

CONTENTS:

Copies mailed to any address in the United States, free of postage, upon receipt of ten cents.

Contents of Dick & Fitzgerald's Dime Song Books.

THE DOUBLE QUICK COMIC SONGSTER.

BILLY BIRCH'S ETHIOPIAN SONGSTER.

Copies mailed to any address in the United States, free of postage, upon receipt of ten cents.

Contents of Dick & Fitzgerald's Dime Song Books.

Copies mailed to any address in the United States, free of postage, upon receipt of ten cents.

THE LITTLE MAC SONGSTER.—CONTENTS

THE TENT AND FORECASTLE SONGSTER.—CONTENTS:

Dick & Fitzgerald's Dime Song Books.

The Heart and Home Songster; Containing a Choice
Collection of Songs of the Affections, and embracing all the most Popular and Fashionable Comic, Convivial, Moral, Sentimental and Patriotic Songs.

CONTENTS:

Billy Birch's Ethiopian Melodist; Containing Fifty-
Nine new Plantation, Comic, and Sentimental Songs.

The Double-Quick Comic Songster; Containing
Forty-Three Comic Songs never before published.

All the Songs in this Book may be sung to popular and well-known tunes.

⁂ Copies of each of the above Song Books, mailed, post-paid, on receipt of TEN CENTS. Send Cash orders to

DICK & FITZGERALD, Publishers, New-York.